AFGHANISTAN
AND CENTRAL ASIA

A MODERN HISTORY

AFGHANISTAN
AND CENTRAL ASIA

A MODERN HISTORY

Martin McCauley

An imprint of **Pearson Education**

London · New York · Toronto · Sydney · Tokyo · Singapore · Hong Kong · Cape Town
New Delhi · Madrid · Paris · Amsterdam · Munich · Milan · Stockholm

PEARSON EDUCATION LIMITED

Head Office:
Edinburgh Gate
Harlow CM20 2JE
Tel: +44 (0)1279 623623
Fax: +44 (0) 1279 431059

London Office:
128 Long Acre
London WC2E 9AN
Tel: +44 (0)20 7447 2000
Fax: +44 (0)20 7240 5771
Website: www.history-minds.com

First published in Great Britain in 2002

© Pearson Education Limited 2002

The right of Martin McCauley to be identified as Author of this Work has been asserted
by him in accordance with the Copyright, Designs and Patents Act 1988.

ISBN 0 582 50614 X

British Library Cataloguing in Publication Data
A CIP catalogue record for this book can be obtained from the British Library

Library of Congress Cataloging in Publication Data
A CIP cataloge record for this book can be obtained from the Library of Congress

10 9 8 7 6 5 4 3 2 1

Cover and text designed by Lisa Glomberg
Typeset by Fakenham Photosetting Limited, Fakenham, Norfolk
Printed and bound in Great Britain by Bookcraft, Midsomer Norton.

The Publishers' policy is to use paper manufactured from sustainable forests.

CONTENTS

CONTENTS

GLOSSARY

al-Qaeda literally 'the base'; Osama bin Laden's international terrorist organisation

ayatollah literally, sign of Allah; term of honour for religious leader of Shiites

Basmachi anti-communist fighters (the forerunner of the mujahidin)

Bolsheviks Russian Marxists split, in 1903, into Bolsheviks (majoritarians) (also called Leninists) and Mensheviks (minoritarians). The former were more radical and willing to use force to achieve communism; the latter favoured a constitutional, peaceful move to communism. Bolshevism (communism) can best be understood as a political religion. They thought they had found the keys to understanding and transforming society through class analysis. The ruling class was the working class.

burqa (burka) Urdu term for clothing which envelops a woman

Commonwealth of Independent States (CIS) association of post-Soviet republics, which does not include the Baltic States (Estonia, Latvia and Lithuania)

Economic Cooperation Organisation (ECO) Iran, Turkey, Pakistan, Afghanistan and the Central Asian states are members

emir Muslim ruler; male descendant of Muhammad (hence emirate)

fatwa a published decision concerning religious doctrine or law

FSB Russian State Security Service (successor of KGB)

GUUAM organisation consisting of Georgia, Ukraine, Uzbekistan, Azerbaijan and Moldova

hadith tradition or report of a precedent set by Muhammad or his early followers

haj the annual pilgrimage to Mecca, to be performed by the faithful once in a lifetime if economically possible

ijma consensus of opinion of the recognised religious authorities at any given time concerning the interpretation and application of the teachings of the Qur'an in any particular situation

imam leader of a mosque. (In Shia Islam 'imam' is the term used for the leader of the whole Muslim community worldwide.)

ishan senior figure in Sufi order, often founded his own Sufi group

Islamic Renaissance Party radical party whose goal was an Islamic republic; strongest in Tajikistan

jihad literally 'an effort of striving'; a religious war; sometimes understood as spiritual struggle

KGB Committee of State Security; Soviet secret police – until 1991. Russian equivalent is State Security Service (FSB)

Khalq faction within the communist party of Afghanistan

khan title of rulers and officials in Central Asia and Afghanistan; historically supreme ruler of Turkic, Tatar and Mongol tribes, and emperor of China, in Middle Ages

madrasa Islamic school

mahdi literally 'rightly guided one', whose return is awaited by Shia Muslims

mekteb elementary Islamic religious school

muezzin the one who gives out the call to prayer

mujahed (pl. mujahidin) one who goes on jihad; Islamic warrior

mullah religious teacher. The term is more common in Pakistan and India

Nagorno-Karabakh in Muslim Azerbaijan but the population is predominantly Christian Armenian; armed conflict began in late 1980s and has still be resolved

Narkomnats the people's commissariat of nationalities, headed by Stalin

NATO North Atlantic Treaty Organisation; founded 1949 to resist Soviet expansion

Northern Alliance anti-Taliban Afghan military coalition

Parcham faction within the communist party of Afghanistan

Pashtun the largest ethnic group in Afghanistan (most estimates give 38 per cent but Pashtuns claim over 50 per cent of the population)

purda literally 'curtain'; the seclusion of women

qiyas analogous reasoning

Qur'an Muslims' holy book

Ramadan the ninth month in the Islamic calendar, the fasting month (usually begins 16 November in the Gregorian calendar)

salām literally 'peace'; a word used as a greeting or salutation

Sharia Islamic religious law; the Urdu word is Shariat

sheikh elder, leader, chief

Shiites the Muslim sect that believes that the rightful successor to Muhammad was Ali, his closest relative; most Tajiks and Hazars are Shiites

sufi mystic

Sunni literally 'one of the path'; orthodox Islam; the majority, who follow the successors of Muhammad by election; most Muslims in central Asia are Sunni; Tajiks are mainly Shiite, as are the Hazars in Afghanistan

Taliban literally 'the seekers'; ruled 90 per cent of Afghanistan, 1996–2001

Tariquat branch of Sufi order, non-violent

Taurah the Torah, the law of Moses, the first five books of the Old Testament

Turkestan literally 'empire of the Turks'; Central Asia

Turkic describes those countries whose languages are based on Turkish; these are Kazakhstan, Kyrgyzstan, Uzbekistan and Turkmenistan. There are Turkic minorities in China, notably the Uighurs, and Afghanistan

Turkmenbashi leader of the Turkmen

Uighurs Turkic people, mainly living in Xinjiang autonomous province, China

ulama group of theologians

umma the world community of Islam, the totality of all Muslims

United Tajik Opposition (UTO) anti-communist militia influenced by radical Islam

Wahhabi (pl. Wahhabien) members of a puritanical reform movement of Sunni Islam founded in the eighteenth century. They are dominant today in Saudi Arabia.

zhu horde in Kazakhstan; there are three *zhus*

WHO'S WHO

Akaev, Askar Akaevich (1944–) a computer specialist with a doctorate in engineering. He was elected president of the Kyrgyz Academy of Sciences in 1989 and, in 1991, the first President of Kyrgyzstan. He was a communist but not a bureaucrat. He became the only new ruler in Central Asia who had not been a communist bureaucrat. At first, he favoured the devel·opment of democracy but the rise of radical Islam disenchanted him with democracy. Much more authoritarian nowadays.

Bin Laden, Osama (1957–) Saudi; the most wanted man in US history, with a reward of up to $25 million for information leading to his capture; fought against the Soviets, 1983–89; set up al-Qaeda, 1989; returned to Saudi Arabia but was disowned; settled in Khartoum but was obliged to leave, 1996; returned to Afghanistan.

Dostum, Abdul Rashid (1955–) general; Uzbek; warlord who controls Mazar-e Sharif; fought with Soviets then against them; then with mujahidin; in exile in late 1990s in Turkey, etc.; important figure in post-Taliban Afghanistan.

Fahim Khan, Muhammad (1955–) Tajik; general, commander-in-chief of Northern Alliance since 2001; trained by the KGB and was deputy to President Najibullah until 1992; changed sides and became chief of NA security when it ruled Kabul, 1992–96.

Karimov, Islam Abduganievich (1938–) Uzbek authoritarian leader who became head of the communist party in 1989. He took the oath as President with one hand on the constitution and the other on the Qur'an. There are no real opposition parties.

Lenin, Vladimir Ilich (1870–1924) one of the most important political actors of the twentieth century; a brilliant, ruthless tactician; he was always leader of the Bolshevik communist group; Leninism is the rule of a party élite.

Namangani, Djuma (1969–2001) an Uzbek; leader of the Islamic Movement of Uzbekistan which is a radical Islamic group; fought in Soviet army in Afghanistan as a paratrooper, then joined the Islamic resistance afterwards. Commanded Uzbek troops fighting alongside the Taliban; killed by an American bomb in November 2001.

Nazarbaev, Nursultan Abishevich (1940–) authoritarian ruler of Kazakhstan who was selected by Mikhail Gorbachev as communist boss in 1989. He was elected President in 1990. He belongs to the middle *zhu* (horde).

Niyazov, Saparmurad Ataevich (1940–) Turkmenbashi (ruler of the Turkmen); the most authoritarian ruler in the region, the whole republic revolves around him. Gas wealth allows him to rule without overt opposition.

Rakhmonov, Imamoli President of Tajikistan since 1994. He ousted the previous communist leader and stayed in power after the end of the civil war (1992–97).

Stalin, Iosif Vissarionovich (1879–1953) brilliant, ruthless political tactician – a better politician and administrator than Lenin. Stalinism is the rule of the party, political policy and government élite – all under the firm hand of the master Bolshevik, Stalin.

ACKNOWLEDGEMENTS

We are grateful to the following for permission to reproduce copyright material:

Adapted political map of Afghanistan, and maps of Kazakhstan, Kyrgyzstan and Tajikistan, Turkmenistan, Uzbekistan reproduced by permission of the Economist Intelligence Unit Ltd, from Economist Intelligence Unit Country Profiles; Map of Afghanistan and pie chart redrawn from *Financial Times*, 26.11.01, reproduced by permission of Financial Times Ltd.

In some instances we have been unable to trace the owners of copyright material, and we would appreciate any information that would enable us to do so.

PREFACE

Afghanistan and Central Asia have been great empires themselves and have been fought over by great empires. Geopolitically, they are the crossroads of east and west. In the past, Genghis Khan swept through and others went on to India and Persia. When China was weak, Russia took advantage and expanded to its western frontiers. Russia wanted to capture India, from the end of the eighteenth century onwards. The route was through Central Asia and Afghanistan. Britain wanted to ensure that Russia was denied an opportunity of turning its imperialist dream into reality. So it invaded Afghanistan so as to get to Central Asia, fighting three unsuccessful wars in the nineteenth century but, at least, prevented the Russians from getting anywhere near India.

The new communist rulers in Russia, in 1919, plotted the invasion of India again. This time the ideology was not imperialist but communist. A treaty was signed with the new Afghan state, in 1921, and this promised to open the route to an anti-imperialist revolution in India and elsewhere in the colonial world. Nothing came of it because Afghans and other Asian peoples did not want to march to communism under the banner of Moscow. They wanted to get there under their own banner. Nationalism confounded the theories of Marx.

The communists tried again, in 1979, to bring Afghanistan into submission but, predictably, failed. The war radicalised

Islam worldwide and led to the emergence of al-Qaeda, headed by Osama bin Laden, the most formidable international terrorist organisation ever to emerge. America had not envisaged this when it trained and armed the mujahidin. When the Soviets left in 1989, the pro-communist President

THE 1979 WAR LED TO THE EMERGENCE OF AL-QAEDA, THE MOST FORMIDABLE INTERNATIONAL TERRORIST ORGANISATION EVER TO EMERGE.

Najibullah remained in power. He was overthrown, in 1992, and executed. The mujahidin were merciless when dealing with their enemies. The problem was that they could not agree on how Afghanistan should be divided up. They engaged in murderous attacks on one another.

The time was ripe for Pakistan and Saudi Arabia to promote a new force, the Taliban. Osama bin Laden's al-Qaeda, provided spiritual and military leadership. In 1996 they took over most of Afghanistan. They then set out to enforce the purest or most fundamental form of Islam seen in the twentieth century. Had they restricted their religious zeal to Afghanistan, they would still be in power. Unfortunately, al-Qaeda had international ambitions. An attack outside the country provoked the

THE TALIBAN SET OUT TO ENFORCE THE PUREST OR MOST FUNDAMENTAL FORM OF ISLAM SEEN IN THE TWENTIETH CENTURY.

world's only superpower, America, to act.

Russia and America are acting in concert to eliminate the Taliban and al-Qaeda but are they following the same agenda? A Russian scholar has said that Afghanistan, economically, is of no importance. Its importance lies in its geographical location. Russia may be fashioning a strategic alliance with India and Iran to keep Pakistan and China out of Afghanistan. There is another reason why Moscow would like to exclude Islamabad. The latter would like to tap into Central Asian oil and gas. Supplies would come through pipelines running across Afghanistan. If Moscow can prevent these pipelines from becoming reality, Central Asian hydrocarbons will have to pass through Russia to reach the outside world. America can no longer rely on Saudi Arabia and the other Gulf states for oil supplies. Within five years Russia and Central Asia can supply America with the oil it gets at present from the Gulf.

All in all, Afghanistan and Central Asia are now of great geopolitical significance. The more we know about them the better.

In order to understand Afghanistan and Central Asia one has to conceive of them as being inextricably linked. Central Asia does not naturally end at the border with Afghanistan. The border was first

IN ORDER TO UNDERSTAND AFGHANISTAN AND CENTRAL ASIA ONE HAS TO CONCEIVE OF THEM AS BEING INEXTRICABLY LINKED.

agreed, in 1780, and then updated by the Russians in the nineteenth century. St Petersburg had penetrated the region and had ambitions to reach India. It may have reasoned that drawing a line between its conquests in Central Asia and Afghanistan would make it easier to defend Central Asia from British incursions. The border placed some Tajiks, Uzbeks and Turkmen in Central Asia and some in Afghanistan. Perhaps the Russians calculated that splitting these nations would afford them the opportunity at some time in the future to propose the union of all Tajiks, Uzbeks and Turkmen – under its control, of course. Whatever the motivation, Afghanistan and Central Asia became Siamese twins. The cultural language of the Tajiks, Uzbeks and Turkmen was Persian or Dari, a variation. The cultural language of the other main ethnic group in Afghanistan, the Pashtuns, was Pashto. These two languages dominate Afghanistan, although there are about twenty main languages. However, the Pashtuns looked east to Peshawar, in modern day Pakistan, their winter capital. The British imposed an arbitrary frontier, the Durand Line, splitting the Pashtun nation and placing some of them in Afghanistan and some in British-ruled India. Uniting the Pashtun nation became an important priority for Afghan rulers, especially after British rule in India ended in 1947. The western border with Iran is also the result of Iran deciding where the frontier should run. Central Asia perceived of itself as Turkestan before 1917. Then Moscow promoted the emergence of separate identities and eventually nations so that today one conceives of Kazakhstan, Uzbekistan, Kyrgyzstan, Tajikistan and Turkmenistan as separate nations and states. Afghanistan never suffered colonial rule for very long and hence has not split into separate nations and states. However, the Tajiks and the Uzbeks, perceive of themselves as the natural rulers of the north and, together with the Hazaras, also Dari speakers, form a barrier to the extension of Pashtun influence in the north. The Pashtuns rule in Kandahar and compete with the ambitions of the Tajiks and Uzbeks in Kabul, the Afghan capital.

About one-eighth of Afghanistan is fertile, indeed much of this land, is very fertile, and it is almost all in the north along the border with Central Asia. The exception is Kandahar which is an oasis surrounded by fields and orchards of luscious fruit and other culinary delights. Kandahar pomegranates were so famous that they appeared on the dinner tables of the British Raj in Delhi. There are deposits of natural gas in the north as well. Indeed it is conceivable that the oil and natural gas fields of Central Asia extend into northern Afghanistan. This is a mouth-watering prospect for the Tajiks, Uzbeks and Turkmen as it would lead to their economic dominance of Afghanistan. Hydrocarbon reserves could be developed in tandem with those of Central Asia. Hence, as mentioned above, Central Asia and Afghanistan are Siamese twins. Another way of looking at them is to think of a hand. The palm is Afghanistan and the five fingers are the Central Asian states.

MAPS

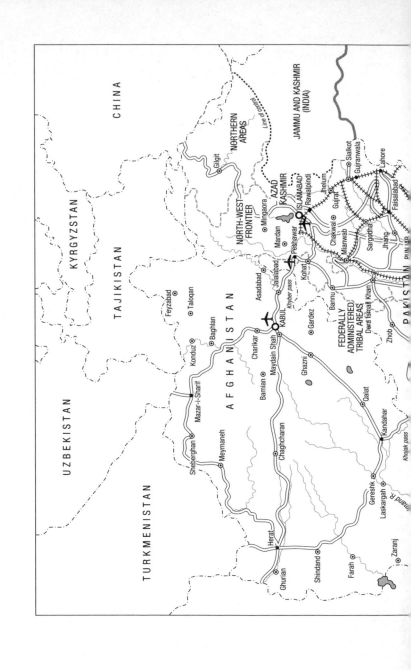

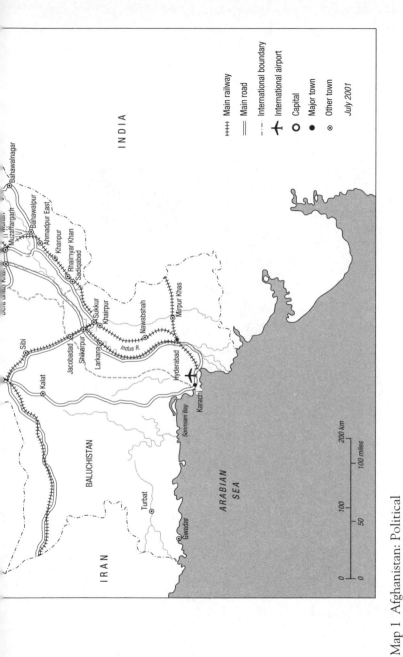

Map 1 Afghanistan: Political

Source: Reproduced by permission of the Economist Intelligence Unit Ltd. Country Profile map for Afghanistan.

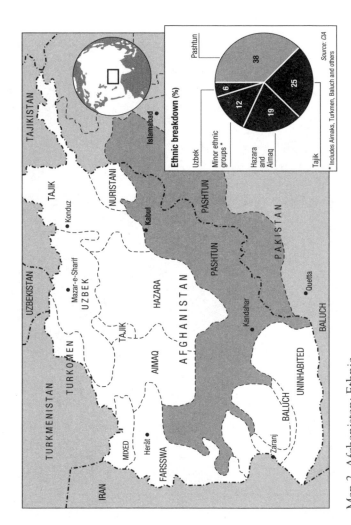

Map 2 Afghanistan: Ethnic
Source: *Financial Times*

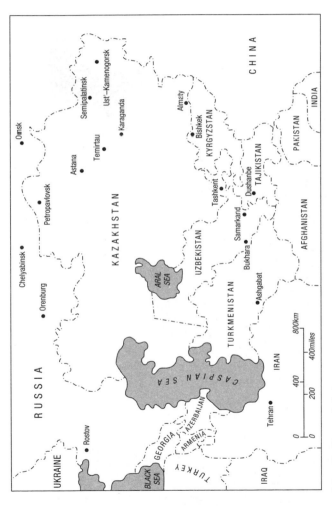

Map 3 Central Asia

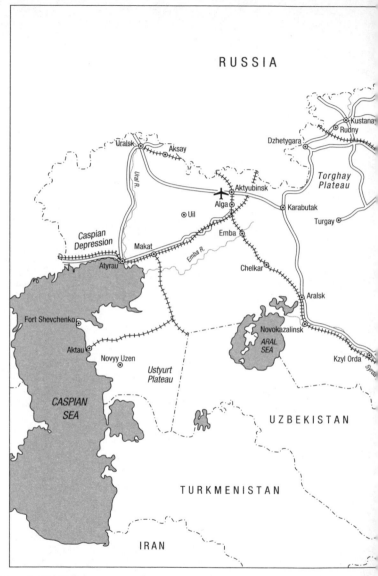

Map 4 Kazakhstan
Source: Reproduced by permission of the Economist
Intelligence Unit Ltd. Country Profile map for Kazakhstan.

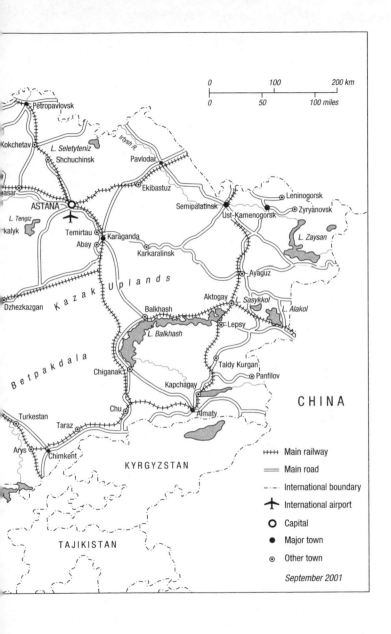

++++	Main railway
═══	Main road
—·—·	International boundary
✈	International airport
○	Capital
●	Major town
⊙	Other town

September 2001

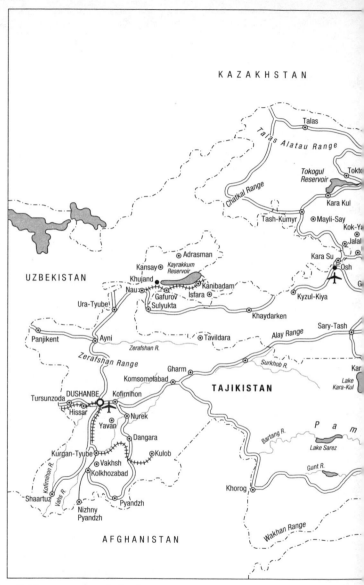

Map 5 Kyrgyzstan and Tajikistan
Source: Reproduced by permission of the Economist
Intelligence Unit Ltd. Country Profile map for Kyrgyzstan
and Tajikstan.

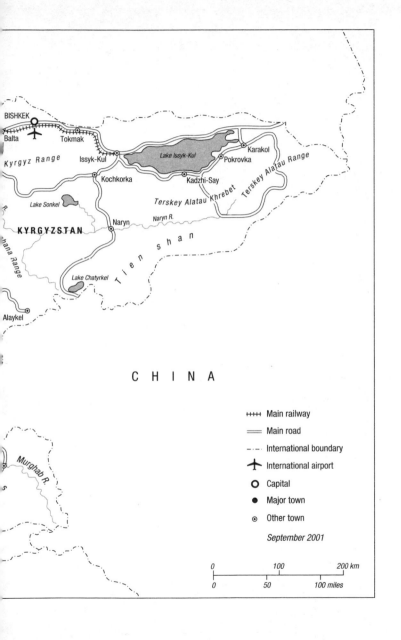

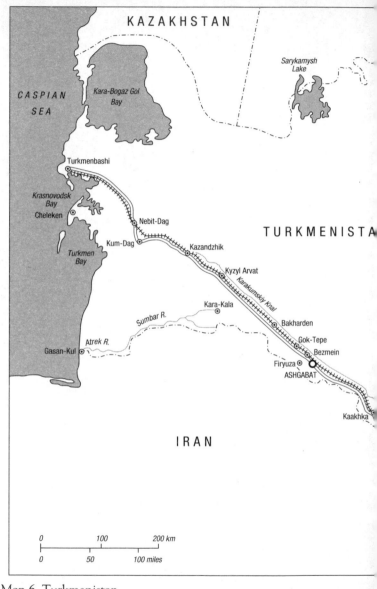

Map 6 Turkmenistan
Source: Reproduced by permission of the Economist
Intelligence Unit Ltd. Country Profile map for Turkmenistan.

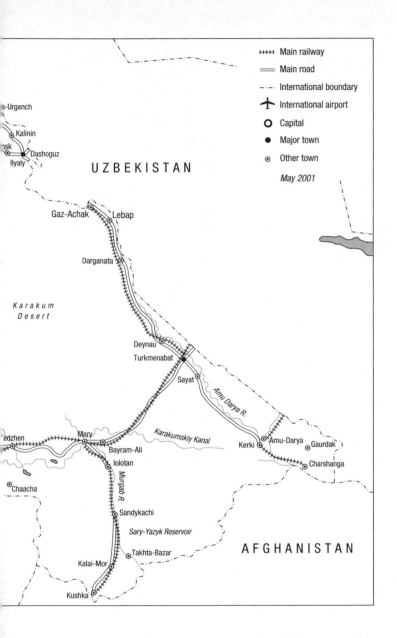

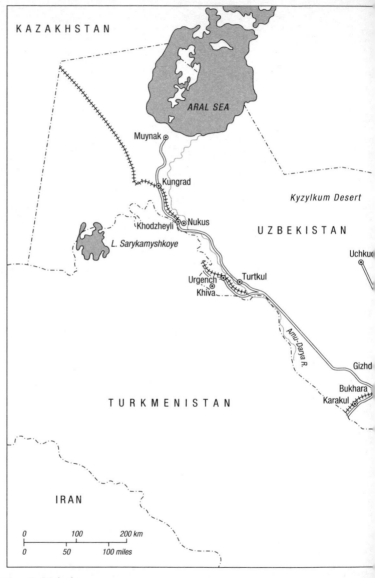

Map 7 Uzbekistan
Source: Reproduced by permission of the Economist
Intelligence Unit Ltd. Country Profile map for Uzbekistan.

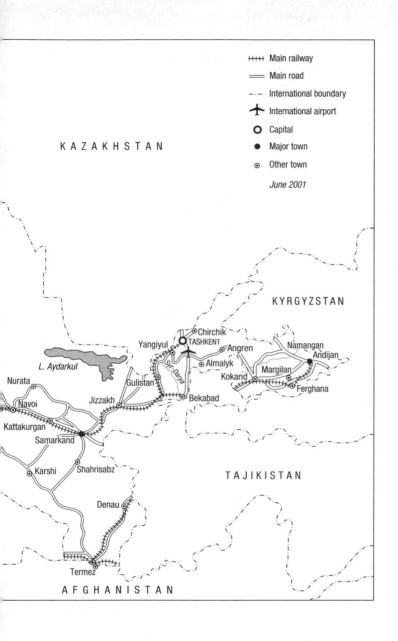

ONE

INTRODUCTION

AFGHANISTAN

Television pictures of Afghanistan portray it as a barren, rocky, mountainous land. The people look undernourished and desperate to find sustenance. Most of all they would like a quiet life after all the strife and bloodshed of the last twenty years or so. Eighty per cent of the country is mountainous. Afghanistan is where the Himalayas end and afford a way north across a plain. The mountains are a blessing and a curse. They have always afforded protection against the foreign invader whose instincts have been consistently predatory. Families, clans and tribes have been able to escape the ruthless scourge of the attacker. However, this led to isolation as a necessary price of survival. Scratching a living from the often inhospitable terrain was very difficult and back-breaking. Why not wait until someone else's harvest was ripe and then seize it? Sometimes there was no choice. If one's own farming was unsuccessful, one was presented with a stark choice. Go out and steal some food or die a lingering death. The history of the ethnic groups in Afghanistan is one of permanent conflict, over resources, food, women, water. Indeed, if there was anything worth having, there was a fight. Almost all societies went through this phase. There may have been some pacific societies which solved all their conflicts by compromise and negotiation but they no longer survive. The history of man is the history of conflict. When women rule there is also conflict.

THE HISTORY OF THE ETHNIC GROUPS IN AFGHANISTAN IS ONE OF PERMANENT CONFLICT.

The ethnic groups in the north of Afghanistan could afford to be less bellicose. Their land was fertile and, when irrigated, provided abundant crops. When the predator arrived, they could not seek refuge in the mountains and wait until he lost patience and left. This would have meant abandoning their food and artifacts. Better to negotiate a tribute and hope he would move on. Sedentary societies are often less belligerent than mountain societies. They are richer and have more to lose through endless conflict. The history of the Tajiks, Uzbeks and Turkmen, in the north, is less violent than that of the Pashtuns and the others in the south. This is not saying much. All the clans and tribes are fiercely independent and find it impossible to unite under a single banner. This is not quite correct, the only banner they will unite under is to expel the foreign infidel who has had the temerity to think he has a right to rule their land. True, this needs qualifying a little. They are all Muslims and this is an

ALL THE CLANS AND TRIBES ARE FIERCELY INDEPENDENT AND FIND IT IMPOSSIBLE TO UNITE UNDER A SINGLE BANNER.

important part of their identity. Even here, they are split
between the Sunnis and the Shiites.

A major reason why Afghans are so fractious is that
Afghanistan is a pre-industrial society. Industrialisation brings
disparate ethnic groups
together to forge an
industrial working class
and a new middle class
emerges. It is different

> A MAJOR REASON WHY AFGHANS ARE SO FRACTIOUS IS THAT AFGHANISTAN IS A PRE-INDUSTRIAL SOCIETY.

from the merchant class which tends to retain family, clan and
ethnic roots. Working together forges a new national identity
which can transcend the old, rurally based identity. There are
reasons why Afghanistan is not an industrial society and these
will be discussed below. For instance, there are no railways. It
is difficult to conceive of industrialisation without railways.

The country resembles a leaf. The Hindu Kush and its extension
westwards (Baba and Bayan mountains, for example) divide the
country in two. There are three distinct geographic regions: the
central highlands, the northern plains and the south-western
plateau. The central highlands have many high mountain peaks
and narrow valleys and some very important strategic passes. The
Kyber pass, for instance, gives access to Pakistan and India, south-
east of Kabul. The northern plains run from Iran to the Pamirs,
near the border with Tajikistan, and are part of the Central Asian
steppe. The Amu-Darya river separates them. There is much fertile land and slowly rising foothills. The area is densely populated
and farmed intensively. Besides agriculture, there are rich
deposits of minerals and natural gas. The south-western plateau
has high plateaux, deserts and semi-deserts. Almost all of

Afghanistan lies between 700 and 3,000 metres above sea level. About three-quarters of the country is inaccessible terrain. Afghanistan has the greatest temperature range in the world, with lows of −50° to highs of +53° Celsius.

Afghanistan has always been strategically important. It is easy to penetrate from Central Asia and leads on to India in the east and Persia and the riches of the Middle East in the west.

AFGHANISTAN HAS ALWAYS BEEN STRATEGICALLY IMPORTANT.

Alexander the Great left his mark in the fourth century BC. After his death the southern part of Afghanistan was ruled from northern India. Islam came to the country in the seventh century AD, but the invaders were unable to hold on to the territory and were soon expelled. Prior to this Hinduism and Buddhism were influential. There were Hindu kings ruling from Kabul. Local dynasties emerged which adopted Islam in the ninth and tenth centuries. The northern part of the country was often ruled from Bukhara, in present-day Uzbekistan. Genghis Khan arrived in 1219, waged destructive wars and carried everything before him. His empire fell apart after his death. Towards the end of the fourteenth century Tamerlane (Timur the lame) conquered large parts of the country. In 1507 the Uzbeks rose to power in Central Asia and made their capital in Herāt, western Afghanistan. All of eastern Afghanistan, south of the Hindu Kush, was part of the Mogul empire, from the sixteenth century. The western part of the

GENGHIS KHAN ARRIVED IN 1219, WAGED DESTRUCTIVE WARS AND CARRIED EVERYTHING BEFORE HIM.

country was ruled by a Persian dynasty, with Herāt as its capital.

The modern Afghan state emerged in the mid-eighteenth century when Durrani Ahmad Shah, a Pashtun, became powerful enough to be proclaimed king. He also ruled in Delhi and Kashmir. Kandahar was his capital, where he is buried, and Peshawar can be regarded as his winter capital. His son moved the capital to Kabul. Hence from its inception, Afghanistan was a Pashtun-dominated state. It was then up to the Pashtuns to enforce their rule throughout the country. Given the large numbers of other ethnic groups and the inhospitable terrain of much of the country, this task proved extremely difficult. Indeed, one can say that Afghans today think of themselves first in ethnic terms and then as together living in a common territory, Afghanistan. Afghan kings were always Pashtuns. Had other ethnic groups, for instance, the Tajiks, provided the king from time to time, a common Afghan ethnic identity might have emerged. It was reasonable that the royal family was Pashtun since demographically Pashtuns dominated the country. The Durrani line ruled until 1973.

Afghanistan found itself between two expanding empires, the Russian and the British. As one Afghan king once ruefully admitted, his country was like a grain of wheat in a flour mill waiting to be ground down by these two millstones. He also likened it to a goat between two ravenous lions. This forced the Afghans to develop great ingenuity and cunning to survive. Tsar Alexander I of Russia, at the beginning of the nineteenth century, planned an invasion of India through

Afghanistan but nothing came of it. Britain's policy was to nibble away at Afghanistan. In 1836 London annexed Peshawar and the surrounding area which was populated by Pashtuns. The following year a Persian ruler laid siege to Herāt. This alarmed Britain which regarded the city as the key to India. The British invaded Afghanistan in 1838 and placed their nominee on the throne in Kandahar. This infuriated the Afghans who cannot tolerate foreign occupation and having a shah imposed on them. Disaster struck, in June 1842, when 4,500 British and Indian troops and 12,000 camp followers were forced to retreat from Kabul. They were all slaughtered. Britain invaded again in 1878 and a permanent British embassy was established in Kabul the following year. Some Afghan territory was annexed by Britain.

IN JUNE 1842, 4,500 BRITISH AND INDIAN TROOPS AND 12,000 CAMP FOLLOWERS WERE FORCED TO RETREAT FROM KABUL. THEY WERE ALL SLAUGHTERED.

Britain now controlled Afghan foreign policy and, in 1893, split the Pashtuns by moving the Indian frontier deep into Pashtun territory. The arbitrary Durand Line was drawn and the Indian side became the North West Frontier Province. London made some amends, in 1895 when, together with Russia, the Vakhan corridor, 150 miles or 241 km long, was unilaterally added to Afghanistan. It linked the country with China in the northeast. The Afghan ruler, Abdur Rahman Khan, was not consulted about whether he wanted to add some more unruly subjects to his kingdom. The reason for Britain's unexpected generosity was that the corridor separated the North West Frontier Province from the Russian-occupied Pamirs.

Abdur Rahman held sway in Afghanistan from 1880 to 1901 and can be regarded as the first ruler to have unified the country. He avoided assassination, a fate which befell several other rulers. His major objective was to ensure as much independence as possible for his country. Britain and Russia came to realise that Afghanistan could serve very usefully as a buffer state. Abdur Rahman had to ensure that the country did not become too attractive economically, otherwise he might face invasion. He ensured that no railways or any major roads were built. The reason was quite simple. The foreign invader would use them to take over the country. Perhaps playing off one great power against the other occupied too much of his time. During his twenty-one-year reign, there were twenty major tribal revolts. He was particularly severe on the Uzbeks and Hazaras but he could only subdue them for a season. Even the brilliantly manipulative Abdur Rahman could not contain the fractious tribal leaders. His son, Habibullah, was willing to risk some modernisation and during his leadership the car, photography and hydro-electric power appeared on the scene.

BRITAIN AND RUSSIA CAME TO REALISE THAT AFGHANISTAN COULD SERVE VERY USEFULLY AS A BUFFER STATE.

In 1914, Berlin exerted considerable pressure on Abdur Rahman to join the Central Powers. After all, Afghanistan's two mortal enemies, Russia and Britain, were on the other side. Muslim radicals wanted a *jihad* or holy war against the infidel. Mindful of the fact that his country was far from Central

MUSLIM RADICALS WANTED A *JIHAD* OR HOLY WAR AGAINST THE INFIDEL.

Europe but very near Russia and India, he demurred. In February 1919, he was mysteriously assassinated and the speed with which his son, Amanullah, took over led some observers to conclude that he was involved in the killing. In May 1919, on the basis that the best way of scotching such rumours was to launch a short war, he initiated the third Anglo-Afghan war. Given the overwhelming superiority of the British forces, the conflict did not last long. However, the war in Europe had sapped imperial British will-power and the peace treaty, in August 1919, conceded Afghanistan complete control over its domestic and foreign policies. This démarche stunned the Afghans. Afghanistan was acknowledged as an independent state at the Paris Peace Conference, in 1919.

Amanullah was greatly taken by the Russian revolution and the high hopes of Central Asian Muslims to gain control over their own destiny. In April 1918, he wrote to Vladimir Lenin, addressing him as the 'High-born President of the Great Russian Republic' and referring to him as his 'great and good friend'. Communist Russian oppression of Central Asian activists who wanted independence gave rise to the Basmachi movement, the forerunners of the mujahidin of the 1980s. Despite the fact that the Basmachis used northern Afghanistan as a base for their raids into Central Asia, Amanullah signed a treaty of peace and friendship with Soviet Russia, in September 1920, which was ratified by Kabul in 1921. Russian gifts included a million gold rubles, 5,000 rifles with ammunition, several aircraft, the setting up of a school of aviation, a gunpowder plant and much technical aid. Russian communists were now copying standard imperialist practice. Money buys influence. However, this was just one move by Amanullah in the great game of chess to secure control of the region. His objective was a confederation of Afghanistan and Central Asia, dominated, of course, by Kabul. In this regard he diplomatically recognised Bukhara and Khiva, in Central Asia, in 1919, in order to establish them as states in international law.

Amanullah continued the modernisation of Afghanistan but at a modest pace. The problem was that the reforms were becoming expensive and his treasury was perpetually short of money. His policies provoked a revolt in Khost, in 1925, and it was suppressed after Soviet and German pilots had flown missions against the rebels. Another treaty with the Soviet Union was signed the following year and one of its objectives was to secure Soviet aid in the eventuality of an internal revolt against Amanullah's rule. The Soviet pilots stayed and Soviet engineers began building a road from Kabul northwards. Soviet advisers began appearing in government offices to advise on policy.

The problem was that reform was proving more and more unpopular. Amanullah decreed that Afghans should wear western dress in Kabul. He also wanted land reform, education for women and the banning of the burka or veil. The country exploded in protest, in 1929, and Amanullah was swept away by a Tajik bandit. The latter lasted nine months and then

AMANULLAH DECREED THAT AFGHANS SHOULD WEAR WESTERN DRESS IN KABUL. HE ALSO WANTED LAND REFORM, EDUCATION FOR WOMEN AND THE BANNING OF THE BURKA OR VEIL.

Nader Shah took over. He immediately put into reverse many of the modernisation measures.

The Second World War offered Afghanistan the opportunity to regain the Pashtun-populated North West Frontier Province. Berlin was quick to promise even more – the frontiers of the eighteenth century Durrani empire. Even Karachi was thrown in. All the Germans wanted in return was for the Afghans to foment unrest in north-west India. The Afghans took time to decide. Then the Soviet Union joined the war against Germany. Britain and the Soviet Union occupied Iran. It had been a wise decision to wait. London and Moscow then demanded that all non-diplomatic Axis personnel should leave Afghanistan. They were promised safe passage but this promise was broken.

Belligerents had a voracious appetite for food and food products, indeed everything that was of use to the war effort. The supply of karakul skins to the London market had been a major money spinner but demand dried up in wartime Britain. However, Afghanistan did export food products and this more than made up for other lost markets. A major disadvantage was that it was almost impossible to import machinery to expand the crop area as countries moved over to war production. This held back Afghan agriculture. Now Afghanistan had resources to improve its infrastructure. In 1946, an American company began work on repairing irrigation dams, building new ones and repairing main roads, all west of Kandahar. This project ran until the late 1970s and devoured resources, including US aid, at an alarming rate. It was an object lesson in the difficulties confronting those who were seeking to modernise Afghanistan.

The establishment of the state of Pakistan, in 1947, was Afghanistan's last hope of regaining its lost Pashtun territories. However, the plebiscite in the North West Frontier Province only presented voters with a choice of becoming part of Pakistan or India. Predictably they opted for Islamabad. Kabul would have preferred a third choice, merging with Afghanistan. This disappointment led to Afghanistan inventing a new state, Pastunistan, which incorporated not only Pashtuns in Pakistan but also the Baluchis in the south-west deserts. It never got off the ground but it did ensure that there was always tension between Afghanistan and Pakistan. Pashtun irregulars crossed the border and attacked Pakistan outposts. Islamabad examined all Afghan lorries and found them defective, thus bringing Afghan foreign trade to a virtual halt. Moscow seized the opportunity and signed a new treaty with Kabul which provided for the duty-free export of goods across Soviet territory. It also promoted the exchange of Afghan agricultural products for petroleum products and other manufactured goods.

THERE WAS ALWAYS TENSION BETWEEN AFGHANISTAN AND PAKISTAN.

Afghanistan now turned to the United States as a counter to the Soviet Union. However, Kabul was rebuffed. Washington did not consider providing Afghanistan with arms and equipment as a worthwhile endeavour. In 1953, the new Prime Minister Sardar Mohammed Daoud – a first cousin of King Zahir Shah and destined to stay in power for almost ten years – made a final effort to secure American backing. His anger knew no bounds when he failed. Afghanistan now chose the Soviet Union as its partner and model for modernisation. This was to have bitter consequences for both Kabul and Washington. Daoud and a few ministers ran the country and only consulted others if they needed advice. Economic development was preferred to political reform and the Soviet Union and Czechoslovakia played the leading roles. Afghan anger at Pakistan boiled over in 1955 when mobs were permitted to loot Pakistani diplomatic missions. American mediation was needed to calm the situation. Washington did provide Afghanistan with some military aid. However, it had to ensure that these arms were not used against Pakistan. Hence aid was limited. In December 1955, the Soviet leader Nikita Khrushchev stopped off in Kabul, the last stop of a triumphal Asian tour (so great was his popularity in India that he was almost crushed to death). He came bearing gifts, an aid package of $100 million no less. He became the flavour of the month in Kabul. The Soviets began constructing airports and a road from Kabul to the Soviet border. Regular flights between Kabul and Tashkent began. During the 1950s, American aid was almost $150 million but Soviet aid was just under $250 million. However, by the end of the 1950s Afghanistan was completely dependent on the Soviet Union for arms and 90 per cent for petroleum products. In 1961 Pakistan closed the border with Afghanistan again and fighting took place on the frontier. This made the country more dependent on the Soviet Union but the border was reopened in 1963.

> KHRUSHCHEV CAME BEARING GIFTS, AN AID PACKAGE OF $100 MILLION NO LESS. HE BECAME THE FLAVOUR OF THE MONTH IN KABUL.

Daoud brooked no opposition to his policies and regarded his ministers as little more than messenger boys. Economic development did take place and this eventually paved the way for Daoud's dismissal in 1963. A developing economy cannot be run by one man, however talented. His departure paved the way for a constitution which was given the royal assent in 1964. It provided the framework for a parliamentary monarchy and a nascent democratic way of life. However, about 90 per cent of the population were illiterate, communications were elementary, organisations which encompassed those outside family and tribal ties were almost non-existent, loyalties and hostilities were local, fierce and consuming and, of course, there was no perception of a common Afghan identity or unity. The sickly plant of democracy struggled to survive in such an environment before it was cut down in 1973. Perhaps one should marvel that it managed to survive so long. Inevitably it was replaced by the traditional Afghan mode of rule, one-man rule.

THE SICKLY PLANT OF DEMOCRACY STRUGGLED TO SURVIVE IN SUCH AN ENVIRONMENT BEFORE IT WAS CUT DOWN IN 1973.

The Soviet Union was going from strength to strength in the late 1950s and early 1960s. Even some in the west began fearing that the communist tide was unstoppable. Not surprisingly, communism was a powerful magnet to those looking for a way out of underdevelopment, poverty and backwardness. Central Asia had made economic and social progress and had left Afghanistan behind. The Soviets had an eager audience for their version of the good life among Afghan students and military in the Soviet Union. Many young men and women in Afghanistan were also eager to embrace Marxism. The People's Democratic Party of Afghanistan (PDPA) – the communist party – was founded on 1 January 1965 in Kabul. The first meeting took place in the home of Nur Mohammed Taraki and, appropriately, he was elected secretary general. Afghan communists owned property and were mainly from the propertied and small middle class. These events were only revealed in 1979 – such was the level of secrecy observed. The party was to prove itself unswervingly loyal to Moscow. Some communists won seats in the elections to the lower house of parliament, in 1966, including Babrak

THE PDPA WAS TO PROVE ITSELF UNSWERVINGLY LOYAL TO MOSCOW.

Karmal. Taraki and Hafizullah Amin stood but were defeated. Karmal led the communist assault on the proposed Prime Minister and his government. He mobilised Kabul students and the riots led to several deaths. This cast a pall over proceedings and a new Prime Minister took office. Given the record of Afghan communists in subsequent years, it is doubtful if Moscow was in control of the situation. It is more likely that Karmal consulted the Soviet embassy, got the go ahead, and then deployed his own tactics.

The personal hostility between Taraki and Karmal led to the PDPA splitting, in June 1967. Taraki became leader of the Khalq (masses) and Karmal headed the Parcham (flag) factions. Ideological differences were minimal as both groups swore loyalty to Moscow. Khalq was predominantly Pashtun while Parcham consisted mainly of other ethnic groups. Moscow did its best to bring the sides together, and even effected a formal reconciliation, in 1977, but it did not last.

This revealed that the ethnic dimension in Afghanistan was so strong that even Marxism, the Marxism of converts, could not overcome it.

In July 1973, Sardar Mohammed Daoud returned to power in a lightning coup, aided by Parcham. The most important element in his success was that he ensured that some members of the instruments of coercion, the military and the police, sided with him. It turned out later that most of them had pro-Soviet sympathies. Zahir Shah, king since 1933, was in Italy at the time and decided to stay there. The constitution was set aside and civil liberties curtailed. Afghanistan became a republic.

THE CONSTITUTION WAS SET ASIDE AND CIVIL LIBERTIES CURTAILED. AFGHANISTAN BECAME A REPUBLIC.

Over half of the ministers in the new government were linked to the PDPA. It is a moot point whether Daoud was aware of this. A fundamentalist Islamic group had been planning to influence events and perhaps the timing of the coup against the king was to forestall an Islamic bid for power. The Islamic group was crushed by the military and the leaders sought refuge in Peshawar, in 1975. Here they plotted against Daoud. The leaders, Gulbuddin Hekmetyar, Burhanuddin Rabanni and Ahmed Shah Masoud were later to lead the mujahidin.

A violent struggle for power developed between Daoud and the Marxists which the latter eventually won, in April 1978. Daoud Khan and most of his family were killed and the communist Democratic Republic of Afghanistan was proclaimed.

The two Marxist factions soon fell out. The new government launched very ambitious social and economic reforms which undermined traditional Afghan values. This led to revolt. The US ambassador, Spike Dubs, was murdered, in February 1979, after being kidnapped by four Afghans demanding the release of some activists. Washington blamed Moscow but its complicity is unclear. The Soviets only had a limited influence in what had become a murderous political environment in Kabul. President Jimmy Carter was outraged and, on 23 July 1979, announced the withdrawal of most US personnel. On 3 July, he had signed the first directive for secret aid to the opposition. Zbigniew Brzezinski, national security adviser to the President, warned him that this would provoke a Soviet military intervention. He was ignored. Moscow, fearing the country would fall under the sway of an American puppet, invaded in December 1979. A blood bath followed and the Soviets helped to wipe out many of the opposition Marxists. They installed Babrak Karmal. He quickly labelled Hafizullah Amin, the previous strongmen, a CIA agent linked to Dubs. This was patently absurd but it justified the killing of Amin. Moscow appears to have lost patience with Amin in the summer of 1979 and then began searching for a credible successor. This is a major reason why so much blood flowed in the second half of 1979. The Soviets eventually concluded that the only way to ensure the country did not fall under American influence was to occupy it. The decision to intervene was taken by the geriatric Soviet leadership, headed by the drug-dependent Leonid Brezhnev. The available documents reveal that the decision was reached after reports by the KGB which were quite positive. The feeling was that it would only take about a month to gain control.

Babrak Karmal could then be manipulated according to Soviet interests. Given that the Soviets had only a tenuous control over the PDPA it is amazing that Moscow believed that it could march in and take control. It did have its own officers in the military and police and all armaments were Soviet. The Soviets appeared to be totally ignorant about Afghan culture. They were bemused when male Afghans refused to be treated by female Soviet doctors. They were blissfully unaware that the

THE SOVIETS APPEARED TO BE TOTALLY IGNORANT ABOUT AFGHAN CULTURE.

country had a deeply embedded Muslim culture. Many Soviet officers took their wives and children as if they were going on holiday. This ended after some Russian women were skinned alive by the rebels. The true horror of what they had unleashed was beginning to dawn on them.

The communist Afghan government after 1973 had attempted to modernise rapidly. Land reform, female emancipation, the abolition of the burka were only some of the measures decreed. It appeared simple to the Afghan comrades. All they had to do was to adopt the same tactics which had succeeded, apparently brilliantly, in Central Asia. As it turned out they proceeded too quickly and the mullahs began to plot their revenge. There was another difference between Central Asia and Afghanistan. In the former, the Russians had used their own troops to achieve overwhelming military success. In Afghanistan they expected the Afghan military to do the fighting – and take the losses – for them. There was another disadvantage. Most of the population of Central Asia live in the plains. Most of Afghanistan is mountainous.

Soviet anger led to their bombing villages and towns in order to drive the population into the cities where it would be easier to monitor them. They hoped this would deny the rebels any support or supplies. The mujahidin became very skilled guerrilla fighters as they were outnumbered and outgunned by the Afghan and Soviet military. Guerrilla warfare was new to Moscow and it never learnt how to counter it.

The vicious, destructive civil war lasted until the Soviets were obliged to leave in 1989. They had poured over 350,000 troops into the country (there were never more than 120,000 at any one time) and had lost about 15,000 dead. The Afghans lost about 1.3 million dead and the same number maimed. The Afghan experience permanently scarred many Russians. It undermined the military as it became involved in drug trafficking and other forms of corruption. So great was the disillusionment that Russians began calling the country (Af) gavnistan (Af-shit-stan). The Soviet people revealed little enthusiasm for the war and returning veterans were given the cold shoulder.

RUSSIANS BEGAN CALLING THE COUNTRY (AF) GAVNISTAN (AF-SHIT-STAN).

Afghanistan was a zero-sum game for America. Anything that hurt the Soviets was good for America. The sooner they were defeated and driven out of the country the better. That would represent a triumph for American policy. Once defeated in Afghanistan, Moscow could be undermined elsewhere. American policy turned out to be a catastrophic mistake, a gigantic Pyrrhic victory. On the basis of my enemy's enemy is my friend, Washington helped bring into being the

most formidable ter-
rorist organisation of
all time. They took all
the Americans offered
them and said thank

ON THE BASIS OF MY ENEMY'S ENEMY IS MY FRIEND, WASHINGTON HELPED BRING INTO BEING THE MOST FORMIDABLE TERRORIST ORGANISATION OF ALL TIME.

you. They then turned their training and weapons on the Americans and the west.

After the expulsion of the Soviets, the Americans walked away. So did other western countries. Pakistan and Iran vied to put in place friendly regimes. Given Afghan history, it was absolutely inevitable that the various mujahidin groups would fall out and begin fighting one another for supremacy. They laid the country waste as a result. President Najibullah, who had held power since the Soviets departed fell into the hands of the mujahidin. He was tortured, castrated, shot and hanged. Burhanuddin Rabbani, a Tajik, then became President in 1992.

The reason for this was that, for the first time in 300 years the

PRESIDENT NAJIBULLAH WAS TORTURED, CASTRATED, SHOT AND HANGED.

Pashtuns were not in control of Kabul. It had been captured by Tajiks, under the command of Ahmed Shah Masoud, and the Uzbek general, Rashid Dostum. Rabbani was their over-all leader. The new government was heavily influenced by Tajiks and Uzbeks and this infuriated the Pashtuns. They wanted to attack Kabul in order to regain control of the cap-ital. This despite the fact that the Prime Minister, Golbuddin Hekmatyar, was a Pashtun. Indeed had the Tajiks and Uzbeks not taken control of Kabul the civil war might have been much less violent. Hekmatyar managed to win over Dostum and the Uzbek changed sides. In January 1994 they launched a ferocious assault on Kabul and eventually took the city. They were not concerned about the destruction, they wanted control. Dostum's dumping of Rabbani was all too typical of mujahidin warlord behaviour. They changed partners with bewildering speed. The sides were too evenly matched for an outright winner to emerge. Pakistan, assisted financially by Saudi Arabia, then began promoting the Taliban and they intervened in 1994 and had taken over most of the country in 1996.

Put another way, had the Taliban not reached the Afghan–Tajik border, the problem of insurgents would not have arisen. Rebels could be trained, move into Central Asia and then return to Afghanistan to seek shelter. It was easy to cross the 125 km frontier.

CENTRAL ASIA

Samarkand; Bukhara; Khiva. These golden names roll off the tongue and flood the eye with images of gleaming golden domes, scorching sand, camels and bearded, turbaned men. Central Asia was part of the legendary silk route from China to Byzantium (Istanbul) and on to Rome. The finest silks in all the orient as well as other priceless artefacts made their slow way to European markets.

CENTRAL ASIA WAS PART OF THE LEGENDARY SILK ROUTE FROM CHINA TO BYZANTIUM (ISTANBUL) AND ON TO ROME.

The region was always shrouded in mystery and captured the fancy of travellers and non-travellers alike. Marco Polo, in the thirteenth century, called Bukhara the 'finest city in all Persia'. Coleridge's 'Kubla Khan' (great thirteenth century Mongol ruler), penned under the influence of laudanum, has stirred the imagination of many schoolchildren.

Central Asia or Turkestan (the land of the Turks) was of considerable geopolitical significance for centuries. The Turks, the Mongols, the Chinese and hordes of others swept through the region into Afghanistan in search of the greater riches of Iran, Iraq, Turkey and Egypt. Turkestan lost much of its significance with the development of the maritime route to the Far East and China. The ship quickly replaced the camel. Today, it has regained its geopolitical significance for two reasons: the war against terrorism and the abundance of oil and natural gas deposits. These are among the largest in the world with Kazakhstan's potential oil reserves immense. If the flow of oil from the Middle East is cut, Central Asia becomes of supreme economic importance to the United States and the west (the United States imports over 10 million barrels of oil daily).

Historically, Turkestan can be divided into eastern and western Turkestan. Part of eastern Turkestan now forms part of the Chinese autonomous province of Xinjiang. Here live Uigurs, Kazakhs and other Muslim Turkic peoples who have been divided by history from their kinsmen and women in Central Asia. Western Turkestan stretches to the Caspian Sea.

Today, Kazakhstan, Kyrgyzstan, Tajikistan, Turkmenistan and Uzbekistan comprise Central Asia which occupies an area of over 1.5 million square miles. This is about half the territory of the United States. The states vary greatly in size. They range from Kazakhstan, the largest, with over a million square miles, to the smallest, Tajikistan, which is just over 55,000 square miles. As far as population is concerned, Uzbekistan is the largest and Turkmenistan, the smallest.

About 60 per cent of the region is desert. The main deserts are the Karakum (black sand) which accounts for 80 per cent of Turkmenistan and the Kyzylkum (red sand) which dominates western Uzbekistan. Much of southern Kazakhstan is also desert. This identifies the key natural resource of Central Asia, water. The region is dominated by two great rivers, the Amu Darya and the Syr Darya, the former rising in Afghanistan and the latter in China, which flow into the Aral Sea. The lands bordering them could be irrigated and whoever gained control over irrigation could enforce his rule. Great hydraulic civilisations developed but, inevitably, attracted the envy of others.

The region was always a battleground between the nomad on his horse and the sedentary population. The nomad's domain was Kazakhstan with its vast steppes. The horse devours much of the surplus produced by nomadic societies. Nomads were always on the lookout for easy prey and sedentary societies found it very difficult to resist them. Settled populations could not devote significant resources to maintaining large numbers of horses. It was economically more rational to pay tribute. Hence the Amu Darya and Syr Darya valleys were a perpetual area of conflict.

Two factors unify the peoples of Central Asia: language and religion. All (except the Tajiks) speak a Turkic language.

They were not **TWO FACTORS UNIFY THE PEOPLES OF**
distinct languages **CENTRAL ASIA: LANGUAGE AND RELIGION.**
before 1917, rather
dialects of Turkish. The Soviet authorities, in order to prevent the emergence of a unified Turkestan, deliberately frag-
mented the region. They set up new states (none of them
existed before 1917) and new languages. For instance, Kazakh
and Kyrgyz were very similar but their division gradually led
to two distinct languages emerging. The Tajiks speak a non-
Turkic language which is close to Persian.

Islam is the dominant religion. First brought to Turkmenistan
in the eighth century by Arab invaders, it was not until the
fourteenth century that it was adopted throughout the region.
Sunni Muslims dominate. The nomadic peoples observed
Islam but religious passion was only found among the sedentary population.

THE MONGOLS

The Turks established themselves in Central Asia in the sixth
century AD. They arrived from Siberia and Mongolia and were
nomads. The Chinese penetrated as far west as Bukhara and
Samarkand in the following century but were quickly dis-
patched by the Turks. Central Asia became a link between
Mongolia and China, India, Iran and Byzantium. Various
other peoples, such as the Uigurs and Kyrgyz, dominated for
periods of time but it was the Mongol chief Genghis Khan's
cavalry which proved irresistible. One of the most astonishingly successful nomads of all time, Genghis left a permanent
legacy in Europe and Asia. The Mongol Empire at one time

ONE OF THE MOST ASTONISHINGLY SUCCESSFUL NOMADS OF ALL TIME, GENGHIS LEFT A PERMANENT LEGACY IN EUROPE AND ASIA. stretched from northern China (they built the Forbidden City in Beijing and were the first ever to introduce paper currency) to Central Asia, Afghanistan, Iran, Russia, Hungary and Poland. The western advance appears to have been triggered by an attack on them by a small-time prince. Once under way they proved invincible in the field and were incensed by the murder of Mongol envoys near Bukhara who had been seeking to establish trade relations. They devastated the flourishing cities of the Amu Darya–Syr Darya valley and northern Afghanistan and in the latter region destroyed the sophisticated irrigation systems. Northern Afghanistan never fully recovered.

The Tatar yoke

Genghis's son Batu Khan turned his attention to Russia and eastern Europe and in 1240 utterly defeated the Russians and drove them from their capital, Kiev. This event was to have momentous consequences for Russia and became a major turning point in its history. The Tatar or Mongol yoke lasted until 1480 and by then Moscow was the capital. The Russians could not cope with the Mongol cavalry and sought refuge in the forests where mounted horsemen could not penetrate. The Mongols terrified the Russians and they are graphically described as monkeys racing over the top of the long steppe grass. The horsemen crouched on their steeds to give this effect. The Mongols carried on into Hungary and Poland and no European army was a match for them. Only the death of the great khan saved western Europe from penetration. The horsemen returned to their headquarters to elect a new great khan, never to return. The Mongol Golden Horde failed to realise that there were richer pickings in eastern and western Europe and instead devoted their energies to subduing Central Asia. The Russian princes were vassals of the Mongols and annually travelled to their capital to pay tribute to the great khan. Wisely, they always made a will before setting off on the journey.

With the Tatar yoke broken, the Moscow princes (they acquired the title of Russian tsars) began their irresistible expansion eastwards. They took the Tatar capital, Kazan, in 1552 and then moved into Siberia. They reached the Pacific at the end of the seventeenth century. The Russians astutely invited the Tatar leaders to join the Russian aristocracy and many accepted. They were then gradually assimilated into the Russian ruling class. Their experience of Asian affairs was of great benefit to the Russian state. Central Asia beckoned but Tsar Peter the Great turned his eyes westwards. The Russians occupied Crimea at the end of the eighteenth century (after the disintegration of the Golden Horde in 1502, the remnants established their capital at Bakhchiserai in Crimea). However it was only after the Crimean War (1854–56), in which they were defeated by Britain and France, that Russia turned its gaze towards Central Asia. Westward expansion was denied so eastward expansion beckoned.

Timur

One of the most colourful leaders in Central Asia was Timur (Tamerlane or Timur the lame), who pushed back the

Golden Horde between the Amu Darya and Syr Darya rivers. In 1398 he invaded northern India and sacked Delhi and then moved west to attack the Egyptians in Syria and the Ottoman Turks. He died in 1405 on the point of invading China. His extraordinary feats are commemorated in present-day Uzbekistan which claims him as one of its founders. However he lacked the administrative skill of Genghis and after his death his territory was fought over by his numerous sons. The victor abandoned his father's capital at Samarkand and set up court in Herat in western Afghanistan. Oriental splendour and great opulence testified to the wealth of his lands. His son, a keen astronomer, ruled in Samarkand and the city became a major centre for the study of astronomy and mathematics. Timur began the tradition of Central Asian leaders setting out to build empires far beyond their home hearths. Needless to say this resulted in great devastation and suffering for those who found themselves in the path of the invading hordes.

Timur's successors fought one another for dominance and were quite incapable of uniting to resist a common foe. The Uzbeks rode down from central Siberia and fell out among themselves. One group separated and became the Kazakhs and the others carried on towards the south and became the Uzbeks. The Kazakhs split into the Great, Middle and Little Hordes (*zhus*) in the seventeenth century. By 1510, all the lands of the Amu Darya–Syr Darya valley and northern Afghanistan were in the hands of the Uzbeks. Their capital was the khanate of Bukhara. There were two other important cities, Khiva and Kokand. To the south, the Turkmen roamed the Caspian Sea littoral and into northern Iran.

There they enslaved the sedentary population and brought them back to Bukhara to work in the oases.

The days of the great nomad empires were drawing to a close. The Mongols, at their peak, could put 200,000 horsemen in the field, an awesome sight. It made them almost invincible. In the seventeenth century the maritime route, linking east and west contributed to the slow decline of Central Asia. The decisive factor was the use of firearms which could decimate and defeat a numerically stronger cavalry army. Cannon was also a formidable weapon. The nomads were roving bandits. They arrived, fleeced everyone and moved on. Those who demurred were often killed or had their property destroyed. The formidable Turkmen roamed along the Caspian Sea and into northern Iran. They discovered that human beings were a valuable commodity and sold them on as slaves. Some of the nomads settled, their chiefs becoming khans and emirs. They found it more profitable to stay in one location and not to devastate the local economy. After all, they needed taxes the following year. There was always conflict between nomad and settler. This was compounded by struggles among the settlers for dominance. Central Asia was never wholly controlled by a nomad or a settler. It was too extensive and diverse. The Russians had little trouble in subduing the local rulers in the

> THE MONGOLS, AT THEIR PEAK, COULD PUT 200,000 HORSEMEN IN THE FIELD. IT MADE THEM ALMOST INVINCIBLE.

> THE NOMADS WERE ROVING BANDITS. THEY ARRIVED, FLEECED EVERYONE AND MOVED ON.

second half of the nineteenth century. The Tsar then became the first ruler to control all of Central Asia.

THE RUSSIANS COME

The nomadic Kazakhs could only offer sporadic resistance to the human Russian tide and by the middle of the nineteenth century the Russians had penetrated to the Syr Darya. The Russian path was smoothed by the suicidal infighting of the small principalities. It was also helped by the heavy-handed rule of the autocratic emirs of Bukhara. They provoked revolts by the peasants and, predictably, it was increased taxation which lit the fuse. Kokand also exploded, in 1845, and again it was over new taxes. These revolts ended the dreams of the emirs of Bukhara to unite Central Asia under their aegis. In 1868, Bukhara became a Russian protectorate, along the lines of British rule in India: the fiction was maintained that the emir continued to hold sway. Russian merchants were already active in Central Asia and were particularly keen to gain a stranglehold over the lucrative cotton trade. Before the conquest Bukhara had processed almost a hundred thousand tonnes of cotton annually. The emir had had almost a monopoly over production and sale of cotton. The Russians expanded the cultivation of cotton but this meant less land under food crops. The shortfall had to be made up by importing food from Russia. The Russians also introduced western lending practices. Usury (high interest rates on borrowed capital) is forbidden by the Qur'an. Now the Russians extended

THE RUSSIAN PATH WAS SMOOTHED BY THE SUICIDAL INFIGHTING OF THE SMALL PRINCIPALITIES.

loans to peasants who could not make ends meet and pay their taxes. The Russians foreclosed when the peasants could not service their debts. There had been moneylenders in Central Asia before the Russians: Hindus and Jews. The Hindus, especially, had a reputation for being smart operators and fast talkers. Every now and then they were clobbered by the taxman and had to start anew. The Jews paid a residence tax and were not protected by the Sharia (Islamic law).

The Russians thought that the emir of Bukhara was fabulously rich. He developed the practice of showering his Russian masters with gifts. This had the advantage of making them dependent on him as they were loath to criticise him for fear of losing their present. Bureaucrats throughout Russia fought one another for the privilege of visiting the region in the hope they would be richly rewarded. Since he was thought to be as rich as Croesus, the emir was invited to invest in every state project in Central Asia. He funded schools, hospitals and charitable organisations. He also marked special events of the Russia Empire and the Tsar's birthday with gifts. They became more and more sumptuous as time passed and peaked in 1905 when he presented the Tsar with a battleship, appropriately named *Emir of Bukhara*. This made a great impression on Muslims inside and outside Russia. They, of course, believed the emir had his own battleship. By 1900, the emir's largesse to Russia was running at about a million rubles a year (£100,000 in the currency of the day).

BY 1900, THE EMIR'S LARGESSE TO RUSSIA WAS RUNNING AT ABOUT A MILLION RUBLES A YEAR.

Before the Russians arrived, the major agricultural hazard in Bukhara was the locust. Some years huge swarms of locusts would devour anything growing above the ground. The defence used by local farmers was to bury part of their harvest annually as insurance. The following year it was dug up and mixed with the new grain. This gave Bukharan grain a distinctly musty smell! When the Russians arrived they promised to solve the problem. They suggested digging a ditch near the breeding grounds of the locusts. When young, they are incapable of flight and during this period they should be pushed into the ditch and buried. The peasants were very sceptical as they were obliged to dig ditches without any reward. It was just another tax. The other problem was that the locusts were too smart and found other places to proliferate. Both the emir and the Russians became more unpopular as a result.

One of the consequences of rural impoverishment, often the result of foreclosure by Russian moneylenders, was a growing population of landless peasants, who became bandits in turn. They did not prey on villagers but on the more well to do. Their booty was then distributed among their families and others in need. In an English context, they were latter-day Robin Hoods. They operated in groups of four or six and once they had robbed, melted back into village life. As a result, the authorities found it almost impossible to deal with them. Others lived in the hills and made lightning attacks on rich targets.

> ONE OF THE CONSEQUENCES OF RURAL IMPOVERISHMENT WAS A GROWING POPULATION OF LANDLESS PEASANTS WHO BECAME BANDITS IN TURN.

There were almost 5,000 recorded attacks by roving bandits in Turkestan between 1899 and 1917. As each year passed the number of attacks increased. Russian officials were a special target. Thirty-eight were killed and 47 wounded between 1901 and 1915. These bandits were the equivalent of present-day urban terrorists.

The Russian revolutions

The Russian revolution of 1905–7 was a watershed for Turkestan. The Russian naval defeat at the hands of the Japanese ended the aura of Russian invincibility. Also the yellow race had defeated the white race, a symbolically crucial event. Russians in Central Asia became quite radical during the revolution but excluded Muslims from their deliberations. They, therefore, began to organise and demanded, among other things, equality with Russians and the establishment of a Muslim religious organisation in Tashkent. This was ignored but they did elect some Muslim deputies to the Russian Duma or parliament. The first steps had been taken to articulate Muslim interests in Central Asia.

Events in 1910 hastened change. A conflict between Sunnis and Shiites in Bukhara escalated and led to a massacre of Shiites wherever they could be found. The conflict appears to have been ignited by the emir's dismissal of Uzbek officials and their replacement by Persian slave officials. The Persians were Shiites and were perceived as favouring their own kind in the emirate. The emir was away at the time and categorically refused to return and intervene. It was left to the Russians brutally to restore order. Those Muslims who favoured reform banded together in secret societies and strove for a more secular world in which the Muslim clergy would play a lesser role. They blamed the Sunni clergy for inflaming relations with Shiites. Inspiration was drawn from the Young Turk movement in Turkey and the example of Tatar activists. The societies set up secret schools (*madrasas*) to educate a new, more open-minded élite. They opposed the use of violence to promote their goals.

Turkestan exploded in 1916. In June 1916 the Tsarist authorities issued an order mobilising Muslims exempted from military service to do agricultural service in the rear. This brought all the Muslim grievances to a head. The Kazakh and Kyrgyz wanted restitution of their confiscated lands (settled by Russians), others thought that a great opportunity now existed to bring down the Russian Empire. The first armed conflict was in July when Muslims attacked Russians and sabotaged railway installations in Samarkand and elsewhere. Pillage and rape spread. A holy war was declared against the infidel. The Russian army put down the rising after a week but the Kazakhs and Kyrgyz carried on their struggle until the February 1917 revolution. The total Kazakh population, in 1916, was just over 5 million. Almost a million perished between 1916 and 1922 and another 400,000 fled to China, Mongolia, Afghanistan, Turkey and Iran.

PILLAGE AND RAPE SPREAD. A HOLY WAR WAS DECLARED AGAINST THE INFIDEL.

THE ETHNIC KAZAKH POPULATION DECLINED BY 2.3 MILLION BETWEEN THE 1926 AND 1939 CENSUSES AS A RESULT OF FAMINE, DISEASE, DEPORTATION AND EXECUTIONS.

The ethnic Kazakh population further declined by 2.3 million between the 1926 and 1939 censuses as a result of famine, disease, deportation and executions. It took the Kazakhs several generations to recover from the slaughter.

Russians and Muslims welcomed the February 1917 revolution with considerable enthusiasm. The Provisional Government promised a liberal solution to the national question but simultaneously was determined to prosecute the war. It decreed an end to national, ethnic and religious discrimination. All citizens were recognised as equal. However, inequality between nations persisted. Its solution to the national question, which also involved a land problem, was to postpone it for consideration by a constituent assembly – which only met after the October revolution but was quickly disbanded by the Bolsheviks.

Soviets or councils sprouted like mushrooms after a shower of rain in Russia and began to run affairs. A Soviet of Workers' and Soldiers' Deputies, which mirrored the St Petersburg soviet, was established in Tashkent, the most important Russian city in Turkestan. However it was entirely composed of Russian deputies. It saw itself as the new power in the land and totally ignored Muslim aspirations.

THE COMMUNISTS COME

Lenin thought he had the answer to the national problem. Suspicion, resentment and conflict were the norm between Russians and non-Russians. Lenin perceived that 'Great Russian chauvinism' was so strong that a unitary state would not work. This chauvinism was amply illustrated by the behaviour of the Tashkent soviet which arrogated to itself the right to decide the future of Muslims – without bothering to consult them. He proposed the self-determination of nations within the Russian Empire. This, of itself, was not novel but what was novel was his willingness to allow all nations the right of secession from the empire. His critics saw this as a recipe for disaster. Lenin himself admitted that Russia could not live without its non-Russian territories. The grain and industrial resources of Ukraine, for instance, were vital to Russia's well-being. Lenin's answer was audacious. Russians had to fight for the right of self-determination of all nations in Russia. This would convince non-Russians that Russians were no longer imperialist. After the victory of the proletariat (working class), the oppressed nations would no longer need to exercise their right to secede. The victory of socialism would lead to nationality being transcended. Workers would all want to be part of one big happy socialist family. This transformation would occur spontaneously, based on the mutual

THE VICTORY OF SOCIALISM WOULD LEAD TO NATIONALITY BEING TRANSCENDED.

trust which the strategy of national self-determination would have promoted. Some readers may assume that Lenin had taken laudanum before he fashioned this theory but he was stone-cold sober. Protests by other Bolsheviks, especially Jews, that Lenin, far from weakening nationalism was, in fact, promoting it, were brushed aside. As time would show, Lenin's nationality policy was to prove one of the greatest political misjudgements of the twentieth century.

Without realising it, Lenin was a Russian nationalist. All those who joined a socialist state would be assimilated and it would become a 'centralised, monolingual state'. Assimilation was Lenin's answer to all national problems, including the most difficult one, the Jewish question. The principal goals of socialism would be the economic, political and eth-nic fusion of all

ASSIMILATION WAS LENIN'S ANSWER TO ALL NATIONAL PROBLEMS, INCLUDING THE MOST DIFFICULT ONE, THE JEWISH QUESTION.

nations. That was the future. Russia at present was a long way from socialism. The long, hard slog of helping the nationali-ties to overcome their minority consciousness had to begin straight away.

Kazakhs (still called Kyrgyz by the Russians) were delighted that they were to be recognised as a nationality. However, there had been a long legacy of conflict over land with Russian colonists settling in the fertile areas. The Kazakhs demanded the return of their ancestral land before they were recognised as a nationality. The Bolsheviks had to fashion a policy which appealed to two disparate groups, the Russian colonists who regarded themselves as the masters and the nomad natives, still smarting from the 1916 rising. A Kazakh Revolutionary Committee was set up in June 1919 and was parachuted in to establish soviet power, paying due attention to the needs of the two communities. The result was violent conflict. Despite this a Kazakh Autonomous Republic was established in October 1920 leaving the Kazakhs and Russians to find a way of living together. The Kazakhs did gain one concession: there was to be no more Russian colonisation. However the existing Russians were allowed to retain their land. An anti-Bolshevik Kazakh national government, the Alash-Orda, was set up but it soon collapsed.

In the rest of Turkestan an original solution was adopted by Moscow. There were two irreconcilable revolutions: a proletarian revolution among Russian workers and soldiers, based in Tashkent, and a nationalist Muslim revolution, led by the educated bourgeoisie, which established an autonomous power base in Kokand. The Turkmen set up a government in the Transcaspian region. The Bolsheviks had little success in promoting revolution outside Tashkent. Faced with Bolshevik hostility, the Turkmen asked British forces, stationed in Persia, to come to their aid. The Bolshevik Party of Turkestan, composed of Russians, found it impossible to promote national self-determination. Such a policy would have swept the communists off the political map.

In May 1920, Muslims proposed to Lenin that an Autonomous Republic of Turkestan be set up and become part of the Russian Soviet Federated Socialist Republic (RSFSR). He watered down their demands but eventually they gained more autonomy than expected. The main reason for this was the distance between Moscow and Tashkent. He was aware that the real problem in Turkestan was not nationalism but relations between Russians and Muslims. However this was only a tactical move by Lenin as he was waiting for the apposite moment to divide up Turkestan into separate Uzbek, Kyrgyz and Turkmen territories.

THE REAL PROBLEM IN TURKESTAN WAS NOT NATIONALISM BUT RELATIONS BETWEEN RUSSIANS AND MUSLIMS.

How then did Moscow attempt to reshape Turkestan? The chosen instrument was the People's Commissariat of Nationalities (*Narkomnats*). It was headed by Iosif Stalin. *Narkomnats* had sections for each nationality. All local demands had to be channelled through *Narkomnats*. In 1921 official representatives of the Republic of Turkestan were installed and were to advise Moscow of local problems via *Narkomnats*. They were also to relay Moscow's wishes to the locals. Soon every significant initiative had to go to Moscow to be resolved. Then federal committees for each policy area were set up. The agricultural committee busied itself with drafting an agricultural code. Land and water (irrigation) were the key Turkestani problem to be addressed. The locals resented Moscow's interference but the fact that it occurred through *Narkomnats*, which represented nationality interests, sugared the pill. On reflection, the Bolsheviks turned out to be sophisticated imperialists. Appearance and reality diverged widely.

The first Soviet constitution came into force in January 1924. It was a voluntary union of sovereign states. It was a federation but in name only. A federation, to Lenin, was a half-way house to a full unitary state. Each republic had its own parliament and government. A federal parliament (bicameral – Soviet of the Union and Soviet of Nationalities) and government sat in Moscow. However the real power in the land was the Russian Communist Party.

Islam and communism share various similarities. Islam is a universalist religion and Marxism is a universalist ideology. One local Muslim proposed that the Qur'an serve as the

ISLAM AND COMMUNISM
SHARE VARIOUS SIMILARITIES.
source of communist ideas.
Indeed, if one regards Marxism as
a political religion there are even
more similarities. However the comrades in Moscow had a
problem. All the communists in Central Asia were Russian.
The party had no recruitment problem. Indeed it was the
other way round. Every Russian bureaucrat and colonist
wanted to join. This led Muslims to set up their own communist party. Sultan Galiev, the most charismatic Muslim
communist, in March 1918, set up the Russian Party of
Muslim Communists (Bolsheviks), independent of the
Russian Communist Party. Lenin wanted more Muslim members in the Communist Party of Turkestan. Locals rushed to
join and were soon in the majority. They then demanded that
the Turkestani Party, affiliated with the Russian Communist
Party, be reconstituted as an independent Turkestan Communist Party. Things were getting out of hand. To make matters worse, the Basmachi, freedom fighters supported by the
local population, attacked Russians and all symbols of Soviet
power. They severely undermined Soviet power in Turkestan.
The bases of the Basmachis were in northern Afghanistan.
After the conclusion of a treaty with the emir of Afghanistan,
in 1921, Moscow was able to move into Afghanistan to
attack Basmachi bases.

Moscow's response was swift and brutal. It declared that the
Communist Party of Turkestan was a regional organisation of
the Russian Communist Party. Wholesale purges followed. In
1922, over 15,000 party members were expelled (the party
had fewer than 20,000 members at the time). The party was
rebuilt, based on class criteria, and sensitive to the population

balance. Workers were Russian and Muslims were peasants. This meant that almost all leading positions were occupied by Russians with Muslims only occupying minor positions. Over 150 Russian communists were seconded from Moscow to assist the process.

Muslim traditions, way of life, social attitudes and law were far removed from the Russian legal system. Islamic law, the Sharia, expressly prohibited foreign influence. The Bolsheviks, in December 1917, abolished the existing legal system and replaced it with people's courts. This proved unenforceable in Turkestan and Islamic courts and people's courts existed side by side. However, gradually the Islamic courts had their jurisdiction restricted and appeals against judgments in Islamic courts could be heard in people's courts. It became very expensive to take a case to an Islamic court. In October 1924, the RSFSR criminal code was extended to Turkestan. Various Islamic practices were outlawed. In September 1927, legislation banned all Islamic courts and their judgments did not have the force of law. Banned officially, Muslim law had now to be administered underground. The imposition of Soviet law led to a marked improvement in the status of women. In public life their rights were the same as men's. Abducting a fiancée

THE IMPOSITION OF SOVIET LAW LED TO A MARKED IMPROVEMENT IN THE STATUS OF WOMEN.

and the payment of ransom became criminal offences. Divorce was by mutual consent and replaced a husband's repudiation of his wife. Polygamy was strictly forbidden and men had to pay alimony. The practice of a widow

THE VENDETTA, A PART OF LIFE IN THE CAUCASUS AND CENTRAL ASIA, WAS DECLARED ILLEGAL.

marrying her brother in law disappeared. The vendetta, a part of life in the Caucasus and Central Asia, was declared illegal.

The communists set themselves the task of ending traditional Muslim education which took place in *mektebs* (elementary religious schools) and consisted of reciting the Qur'an. The *madrasas* trained a small number of students. The great majority of the population remained illiterate. The communists introduced changes slowly because of the fierce resistance of the Islamic clergy to any form of secular education.

With the weight of centuries of tradition, the Bolsheviks were not going to transform attitudes in Central Asia overnight. How did they set about doing so? They organised

THE BOLSHEVIKS WERE NOT GOING TO TRANSFORM ATTITUDES IN CENTRAL ASIA OVERNIGHT.

the 'indignant masses' who attempted to stamp out vestiges of tradition which had been outlawed. If they found a woman on the street with a

veil, she was forcibly unveiled. They monitored weddings and were particularly keen to stop the coming together of old men and young girls – marriages which had been arranged by the girls' parents. The 'indignant masses' roamed Turkestan enforcing modernisation whether the locals wanted it or not. Another ploy by the Bolsheviks was the setting up of women's sections by the communist party. Females were the most difficult to reach and the women's sections soon appeared in every work-place and social organisation. They also set up women's clubs which flourished for a while since they followed the traditional separation of the sexes. The Komsomol, the communist party's youth organisation, engaged in many recruitment drives. They were very successful but failed miserably when it came to enrolling girls – a major success indicator. Less that 5 per cent of Komsomols in Central Asia were female.

In the early 1920s the peoples of Central Asia shared two ambitions. One was the formation of a pan-Turkic state, Turkestan. The other was the emergence of three political entities based on the steppe nomads (Kazakh–Kyrgyz); the sedentary peoples of the Amu Darya–Syr Darya valley, centred on Bukhara, Khiva and Kokand; and the Turkmen people. The Bolsheviks set about frustrating these ambitions. In 1925, they set up socialist republics, autonomous republics and autonomous oblasts to promote political and cultural diversity. The Kazakhs and Kyrgyz were separated. Since there was no accepted Kyrgyz language, a dialect of Kyrgyz was chosen and declared to be the national language.

The Uzbeks and Tajiks were divided. In many ways this was reasonable as Tajiks spoke Persian. This, however, flew in the face of tradition as Persian had been the political and cultural language of the Uzbeks before 1917. The mosaic of ethnic groups proved a headache but also an opportunity for the communists. The Karakalpaks, very close to the Kazakhs and Uzbeks in tradition, were fashioned into an autonomous republic and placed in Kazakhstan, in 1924. Soon afterwards they found themselves in Uzbekistan. Karakalpak, a local dialect without a written form, was designated a national language. The problem was that very few people used it, as the languages of communication there were Kazakh and Uzbek. The Uigurs and Dungans (Chinese-speaking Muslims) were endowed with cultural institutions. The tactics adopted by the communists gradually became clear. The first stage of the transformation was to ensure that the nomads became sedentary and then when everyone had settled down the key transformation, the move to socialism, would be set in motion.

> WHEN EVERYONE HAD SETTLED DOWN THE KEY TRANSFORMATION, THE MOVE TO SOCIALISM, WOULD BE SET IN MOTION.

During the 1920s the Bolsheviks called on all colonial peoples to rise up in revolt against their imperial masters. The anti-colonial revolution was taken seriously by Russian historians. They presented Russia's expansion over four centuries as one of unmitigated disaster for the natives. Wherever Ivan went rape, pillage, desecration, murder, mayhem and destruction were bound to follow. Russia apologised for its previous sins of empire. The corollary of this was that all opposition to Ivan's jackboot was legitimate and was glorified. Logically this meant that Russians no longer had any right to guide the new nations to a brighter future, they would do that themselves.

> WHEREVER IVAN WENT RAPE, PILLAGE, DESECRATION, MURDER, MAYHEM AND DESTRUCTION WERE BOUND TO FOLLOW.

STALIN'S REVOLUTION

In retrospect, the 1920s were golden years. The 1930s saw the death of national political and cultural élites. Stalin brooked no opposition in his drive to achieve rapid industrialisation and collectivisation. Anyone who attempted to hold back the tide faced annihilation. History was rewritten. The Russians were a great civilising force and those who opposed them obscurantists. Land reform had broken up the large holdings and benefited many landless and small farmers. The land was now collectivised and the large holdings reappeared. Almost all important national leaders in Central Asia were executed on trumped-up charges. This also affected the communist party. Most of the great national writers disappeared. The promotion of nations and national cultures turned out to be tactical. It had brilliantly succeeded in destroying the power of the former rulers and clerics. Now a Soviet élite, appointed by and beholden to Stalin, could replace national élites. Henceforth the second secretary of the communist party was always a Russian or Ukrainian and the head of the KGB also. These men ruled the land.

ALMOST ALL IMPORTANT NATIONAL LEADERS IN CENTRAL ASIA WERE EXECUTED.

Culture was to be national in form, socialist in content. In effect, this meant that paeans of praise to Stalin were expressed in the local language. The Stalin cult blossomed and all that was good emanated from him. The Russian now became the elder brother and

THE STALIN CULT BLOSSOMED.

the natives younger brothers. Anyone who demurred was accused of bourgeois nationalism and sent to the gulag (forced labour camps).

The purges were turned off like a tap in 1938 by Moscow. There was a little respite before the German attack in June 1941. No part of Central Asia was occupied by the Germans or their allies. One Kazakh confided after the war that had the Germans penetrated the region the locals would have slit the throats of every Russian they found. In 1944, a new wave of immigrants arrived. They were members of the over fifty nationalities deported by Stalin from European Russia and the Caucasus. Whole nations, such as the Chechen and Ingush, were packed off east in appalling conditions. Over one-third of the Chechens died en route. An Ingush told me that the cattle trucks in which they were travelling halted in the Kazakh steppe, miles from any village. Everyone was turfed out. Then the train moved on leaving them to dig holes in the inhospitable steppe in search of protection from the bitter night cold. Several million deportees were deposited in western Siberia, Kazakhstan and Uzbekistan with a few elsewhere. All Volga Germans were among the deportees. No distinction was made between communist party members, officers and men in the Red Army and others who had demonstrated their loyalty to the Soviet state. They were all labelled traitors.

Under Khrushchev the deported nationalities were rehabilitated and in 1969 could return to their former homelands. This did not apply to the Volga Germans and the Crimean Tatars. The reason was that their homes and property had been sequestrated by Russians and Ukrainians. The Crimean Tatars bitterly resented this injustice. In Tashkent, Uzbekistan in the early 1970s the Crimean Tatars controlled, among other things, the local meat trade. This black market was, of course, illegal. In Uzbekistan, also in the early 1970s the Basmachis were regarded as freedom fighters and heroes. The Russian claim that the nationalities problem had been solved was self-delusion.

Stalin, in deporting so many to Central Asia, had shot himself in the foot. The Chechens, Ingushi and other Caucasian peoples had their own organised crime networks before deportation. In Central Asia they were able to fashion new networks and link up with the natives and

STALIN, IN DEPORTING SO MANY TO CENTRAL ASIA, HAD SHOT HIMSELF IN THE FOOT.

the local Russian mafiosi. This formed the basis of the formidable organised crime networks which developed under Leonid Brezhnev (1964–82) and then surfaced under Mikhail Gorbachev. They were then given the sobriquet mafia.

THE 1970s: UZBEKISTAN

Although many Uzbeks looked like Italians with deep tans, some citizens with epicanthic (Asiatic) eyes are also Uzbek. Their lineage goes back to Genghis Khan. Another group related to them are the Hazaras who live in central Afghanistan, mainly between Herāt and Kabul. They were persecuted by the Taliban (partly because they are mainly Shiites). Other Hazaras live in northern Iran and in

Baluchistan, Pakistan. Genghis Khan's horsemen left a lasting impression.

Silkworm farms produced all their own food and indeed almost everything they needed. Most of the scientists doing research on silkworms were young Korean women. Farms attempted to be self-sufficient and had a large number of workers. The Korean minority managed to climb the educational ladder quickly.

In the 1970s none of the wine and dried grapes was marketed. It was consumed at party and government banquets and celebrations. Two worlds coexisted side by side: that of the bosses and that of the rest. The nomenklatura or ruling class ran the republic as a personal fiefdom.

KHRUSHCHEV AND THE VIRGIN LANDS

Kazakhstan

Kazakhstan experienced four waves of Russian colonisation. Between 1881 and 1914 over 20 million ha of virgin land, mainly in the steppe, was brought under cultivation. To the Kazakh nomad this was 20 million ha less to roam and feed his horses. The next advance took place during the early 1930s. There were an estimated 3 million nomadic families (10 million persons) in 1917. In 1935, this was down to 450,000 families (2 million persons). Another wave of Slav immigration followed the expansion of heavy industry – mining, steel and machine building – in northern Kazakhstan in the 1930s. Then came Khrushchev who thought the sol-

ution to the country's perennial food problem was to plough
up millions of hectares of virgin land in northern Kazakhstan.

Over the years
1953–64, over 34
million ha were
cultivated. This
extraordinary ex-
pansion was ill-

**KHRUSHCHEV THOUGHT THE SOLUTION TO
THE PERENNIAL FOOD PROBLEM WAS TO
PLOUGH UP MILLIONS OF HECTARES OF
VIRGIN LAND IN NORTHERN KAZAKHSTAN.**

judged and wasteful. In reality, about 12 million ha was
immediately abandoned. Water and wind erosion caused
enormous damage.

Khrushchev launched the scheme without having visited
Kazakhstan. Hundreds of thousands of young, idealistic
Komsomols were recruited to farm the inhospitable steppe.
Needless to say very few of them knew anything about agriculture. The President of Georgia, Eduard Shevardnadze,
was among them. He was polite when he said that organisation was a 'shambles'. Many youths could not stand it and
returned home as quickly as possible. Nevertheless millions
of tonnes of grain were produced, at high cost, and added
to the Soviet diet. Drought was always a constant com-
panion and when the crops failed in 1963 Khrushchev
took the momentous decision to buy grain from the United
States. Under Brezhnev, the Soviet Union gave up trying
to be self-sufficient and imported huge amounts of grain
and other foodstuffs from the United States and other
countries.

THE GREAT UZBEK COTTON SCANDAL

FALSIFYING STATISTICS DEVELOPED INTO AN ART FORM IN THE SOVIET UNION. Falsifying statistics so as to fulfil and overfulfil the plan developed into an art form in the Soviet Union. One of the masters was Inamzhon Usmankhodzhaev, communist boss of Uzbekistan. He and others decided that the easiest way of meeting the ever-increasing plans for cotton production was simply to report to Moscow that the plan had been fulfilled. If the gap between production and plan was half a million tonnes then everyone involved, from picking the cotton to delivering it to cotton mills had to be bribed. Where was the money to come from? The state would pay for the mythical half a million tonnes of cotton so there would be a quite considerable slush fund. This stunningly simple scam was worked during the 1970s and 1980s and involved government ministries, factories and the KGB. The Soviet deputy minister of internal affairs, General Nikolai Shchelokov, one of Brezhnev's buddies, and the deputy head of the KGB, General Semon Tsvigun, Brezhnev's brother-in-law, were involved. Brezhnev protected them while he was Soviet boss (until 1982) but his successor, Yury Andropov, took a dim view of corruption. Shchelokov and Tsvigun were dismissed and died soon afterwards, probably by their own hand. The Usmankhodzhaev case was a national scandal and the communist party agonised over whether he should put him on trial. The risk was that the proceedings would merely confirm the average citizen's view that the Soviet nomenklatura was totally corrupt. Eventually Gorbachev gave the go ahead and Usmankhodzhaev got twelve years, in December 1989.

Among the startling revelations was that after he was arrested, a large number of brown envelopes, stuffed full of rubles, were found in the oddest places, usually behind some item of furniture. This revealed that the poor comrade had received so many bribes he did not know what to do with the money! The story went that when Shchelokov visited Uzbekistan on a tour of inspection he was simply asked how much money he wanted. He then went back to Moscow with sackfuls of rubles.

> THE POOR COMRADE HAD RECEIVED SO MANY BRIBES HE DID NOT KNOW WHAT TO DO WITH THE MONEY!

COMETH THE HOUR, COMETH GORBACHEV

After a series of geriatric leaders, Gorbachev cut a fine figure. He was quite unaware of the parlous state of the Soviet economy and thought that it was like an engine which required a

> AFTER A SERIES OF GERIATRIC LEADERS, GORBACHEV CUT A FINE FIGURE.

good service. Perestroika (restructuring) soon developed into katastroika (catastrophe). Glasnost (openness) allowed suppressed national and ethnic tensions to surface. Gorbachev's increasing difficulties were music to the ears of the ruling groups in the republics. Moscow passed greater decision-making powers to the regions and the locals seized them with both hands. Just how things had changed was underlined by the ethnic riots which followed the dismissal of the Kazakh communist boss, Dinmukhamed Kunaev, in late 1986. He had been a close buddy of Brezhnev and even cultivated the latter's beetle eyebrows. Kunaev was a byword for corruption. His favourites were rewarded with stays at health spas

KUNAEV WAS A BYWORD FOR CORRUPTION.

where every type of luxury was available, including beautiful girls. There were various grades of resorts. Juniors had to do with a few luxuries and a few girls, the middle ranks did a little better and the bosses enjoyed a little bit of paradise. Gorbachev decided that a Russian broom was needed to clean up Kazakhstan. He installed Gennady Kolbin and the riots began. They were racial. Kazakhs regarded Kolbin as an insult to their dignity. Soon Nursultan Nazarbaev took over and normal service was resumed. Gorbachev ruefully concluded that the days of parachuting in a Russian or Ukrainian party boss to run Muslim republics were over. Ethnic violence visited Kyrgyzstan, in June 1990, in Osh, the country's second largest city and the largest market in the Fergana valley. Clashes between the Uzbeks, who were in the majority, and Kyrgyz migrating to the town, left over 200 dead. In 1989 and 1990 there were violent ethnic clashes in the Fergana valley, in Uzbekistan.

THE RUSSIANS GO

The Russian Empire and its successor, the Soviet Empire, passed away in December 1991. Gorbachev's attempt at forging a new Union of Sovereign States failed. Had it not been for the attempted coup in August 1991 it might have come into being. The coup killed it and made Boris Yeltsin

GORBACHEV'S ATTEMPT AT FORGING A NEW UNION OF SOVEREIGN STATES FAILED.

the hero of the hour. The Baltic States were determined to gain independence and believed they were capable of competing in the modern world. Not so the Muslim republics. They were all Soviet creations and as such had never existed as sovereign states. They wanted a close relationship with Russia since economically and militarily they were quite incapable of surviving very long on their own. Russia had a choice. It could create a single economic space for all post-Soviet states (excluding the Baltic States) that could move to a market economy together. However it could also go it alone and dump the others. This is what it decided to do arguing that the others would slow down the Russian race to the market. Gaidar and shock therapy took over. Once this had been decided Russia could dispatch the Soviet Union and President Gorbachev to the dustbin of history. President Nazarbaev of Kazakhstan was invited by President Yeltsin to join the team (Russia, Belarus and Ukraine) which was going to dissolve the Soviet Union and set up the Commonwealth of Independent States (CIS). He accepted but then got cold feet. He still backed Gorbachev but was not perceptive enough to realise that Yeltsin was the coming man and that Gorbachev was the going man. In Almaty, the Kazakh capital, in late December 1991, eleven states signed the CIS agreement.

A NEW DAWN

Had the Bolshevik regime collapsed in the early 1920s, leaders in Central Asia would have attempted to set up a collectivist dream, Turkestan. In 1991, when the Soviet Union collapsed, the agenda was quite different. The communists had succeeded beyond their wildest dream in sowing division

and separateness in the region. New power élites had emerged and they were unwilling to sacrifice anything to the collective good. Why had these élites become so ensconced, given that Moscow dominated the Soviet Union?

> THE COMMUNISTS HAD SUCCEEDED BEYOND THEIR WILDEST DREAM IN SOWING DIVISION.

Nikita Khrushchev (1953–64) was a dynamic and innovative Soviet leader who took on the new nomenklatura, and lost. The ruling class, formed under Stalin, consisted of the party, government, KGB and military élites. He realised that the party and government élites were a barrier to increased efficiency and he sought to make them more accountable to Moscow. He decreed reform after reform which antagonised them to the extent that they colluded against him in a coup in 1964 and removed him. Leonid Brezhnev (1964–82) was the main beneficiary, but he lacked the will and ambition to take on the ruling élites. He struck a deal with the bosses: if they remained loyal to him he would allow them to feather their nests.

In Central Asia, native élites gradually took over. They pandered to Brezhnev's ego, correctly perceiving him a vain, shallow man. One of the masters of this game was Dinmukhamed Kunaev who bossed Kazakhstan. Gorbachev tried to shake up the region when he discovered that its leaders had little interest in perestroika. The Almaty riots of December 1986 ended that démarche. The imprisonment of the Uzbek boss, Usmankhodzhaev, and the posthumous disgrace of his predecessor, Sharaf Rashidov (leader from 1959 to 1982), merely demonstrated Moscow's lack of control.

Hence in 1991 locals ruled Central Asia. They divided up power according to family, group, clan and tribal criteria (in Kazakhstan according to *zhus* or Hordes). In the successor states, only in Kyrgyzstan did the communist élite fail to retain power. Only in Tajikistan was there a civil war to decide who could exercise power. The communists won.

Kazakhstan

In Kazakhstan, Nursultan Nazarbaev, was faced with the problem that Kazakhs only made up about 40 per cent of the population. Russians and Ukrainians combined accounted for 43 per cent. Of the rest, Germans made up 6 per cent. Russians and Ukrainians dominated heavy industry and mining. The Virgin Lands scheme had brought in many Slav farm workers. Nazarbaev's chief objective became maintaining the territorial integrity of his republic. The next was to fashion a political system which placed power in the hands of Kazakhs. He had to be mindful of the fact that the division of power among the Kazakhs reflected the relative influence of the three *zhus*. He is a member of the Middle *zhu* (numbering about 4 million and the most Russified). It was not an accident that the capital was moved from Almaty (Great *zhu* territory – there are about 2.5 million, many of them in south Kazakhstan) to Astana (where the Middle *zhu* are influential). The Little *zhu* count about 700,000 members, but inhabit areas rich in oil and natural gas. Economic development came third. Hence technical competence was not the main criterion in making appointments. President Nazarbaev – in effect President for life – responds, from to time, to criticism about slow economic progress and widespread poverty by sacking his Prime Minister. Three were sent packing during the 1990s. One of them, Akezhan Kazhegeldin (1994–97), the main opposition leader, was convicted, *in absentia*, of corruption and abuse of office.

THREE PRIME MINISTERS WERE SENT PACKING DURING THE 1990S.

Kyrgyzstan

In Kyrgyzstan, the communist party's inability to contain ethnic violence, culminating in the Osh riots of June 1990, undermined its authority. As a result, Askar Akaev, a physicist, was elected President in October 1990 and confirmed in office after the republic's independence. Initially he revealed some enthusiasm for democracy but has gradually become more and more autocratic. This trend culminated in various opposition groups being banned and the imprisonment of Feliks Kulov, the main challenger for the presidency.

Tajikistan

Tajikistan is the only Central Asian state to have suffered a debilitating civil war. The incumbent communist leader, Kakhar Makkhamov, was removed in the wake of the attempted coup in August 1991. Rakhmon Nabiev took over. The new boss had no time to stabilise his position before Tajikistan was forced to go independent. In November 1992, Imamoli Rakhmonov was made head of state by the communist government. This led to widespread civil war which was, in essence, between two regional groups, those from the north (Leninabad, now Soghd) and those from the south (Kulob). The waters were muddied by the emergence of the Islamic Renaissance Party (IRP) with its goal of an Islamic republic. It had considerable support in the east of the country. Fighting devastated villages and rural areas and led to thousands fleeing into Afghanistan. There the United Tajik Opposition (UTO) formed and returned to claim parts of east Tajikistan. International mediation brought the destructive civil war to an end in June 1997. The new coalition was to include IRP members and other opposition groups. Rakhmonov remained President. Most of the east of the country is beyond Rakhmonov's control. Part of the peace deal was to give some lucrative government and business positions to UTO leaders. For instance, Mahmadruzi Iskandarov now heads the state-owned Tajik gas. The ethnic Uzbek minority are not permitted to form political parties. In November 1998, hundreds of armed men invaded Soghd province from Uzbekistan. Tajik troops and the UTO managed to crush the uprising. Tajikistan accused Uzbekistan of being behind the incursion. Parliamentary elections in early 2000 resulted in the President's party, the People's Democratic Party, winning a majority in both houses. The IRP and other opposition parties got just over 10 per cent. The 1997 peace agreement assures the opposition of 30 per cent of posts in the government.

Turkmenistan

Turkmenistan is a fairy-tale land ruled by a fairy-tale prince, Saparmurad Niyazov, who styles himself Turkmenbashi, the leader (in German Führer: appropriate as the country is the size of Germany) of the Turkmen. Bashi has successfully ensured that Turkmenistan is a haven of tranquillity in the sea of Central Asia politics. The country is neutral and maintained measured relations with the Taliban. It is gas-rich and can afford to avoid entanglements. Bashi is everywhere. His portrait is on every building in the capital, Ashgabat, his gold and bronze bust adorns every crossroads, his visage is on every stamp and banknote, in every schoolroom, on the first page of every book published in the country and on every vodka bottle. Television appears only to consist of paeans of praise to Bashi and his indefatigable efforts to improve the lot of his subjects. Those who want to get on carry a small gold head of the Bashi around with them. They think it will bring them luck. The pièce de resistance is a mock Eiffel Tower in the centre of Ashgabat crowned with a twelve-metre high gold statue of Bashi. He holds out his arms and moves with the sun so that his face always radiates its brilliant light. He is the sun king. Nearby is a Madonna-like statue of his mother who died in the Ashgabat earthquake of 1948.

BASHI HAS SUCCESSFULLY ENSURED THAT TURKMENISTAN IS A HAVEN OF TRANQUILLITY IN THE SEA OF CENTRAL ASIA POLITICS.

On festive occasions, Bashi likes everyone to shout: 'Halk, Vatan, Turkmenbashi' (One people, one empire, one leader: in German it is 'Ein Volk, ein Reich, ein Führer': Hitler delighted in this greeting). Bashi cultivates

ON FESTIVE OCCASIONS, BASHI LIKES EVERYONE TO SHOUT: ONE PEOPLE, ONE EMPIRE, ONE LEADER.

Turkmen nationalism. The minister of culture was berated for allowing a school history book to state that in the past other peoples as well as the Turkmen had lived in Turkmenistan. As far as Bashi is concerned, Turkmenistan has always been inhabited by the Turkmen and it is the world's oldest civilisation. The director of the Technical University was sacked for uttering three words of Russian in response to an impromptu question. A small cloud appeared on Bashi's horizon in late 2001. Boris Shikhmuradov, Turkmen ambassador to China and a former foreign minister and deputy Prime Minister, defected to Russia and poured vitriol on his former boss. Are Bashi's days numbered?

Uzbekistan

President Islam Karimov rules Uzbekistan with an iron hand. He became communist boss in 1989 and ensured his own election as President of the republic, in December 1991. He drove his opponent, head of a secular nationalist party, into exile. Other secular political leaders were also forced to move abroad. Islamic opposition gradually developed, especially in the crowded Fergana valley, in response to poverty and repression. The Islamic Movement of Uzbekistan (IMU), a banned organisation, and which only surfaced in April 1999, is now the major focus of religious opposition. The IMU is linked to the Taliban and has engaged in armed conflict with the governments of Uzbekistan and Kyrgyzstan. There have been various attempts on President Karimov's life, as he has a host of enemies. In January 2000, he was reelected President with the only other candidate publicly voting for him.

TWO

THE ECONOMY: BIG BUCKS AND WHO GETS THEM?

AFGHANISTAN

The population of Afghanistan, in 2000, was 25.8 million. About 1.3 million were killed during the war against the Soviet Union and as many again maimed. About 6 million fled to Pakistan and Iran with many returning. In November 2001, the UN estimated that there were 2 million refugees in Pakistan, 1.5 million in Iran, 1,500 in Turkmenistan, 8,800 in Uzbekistan and 15,400 in Tajikistan. It can be assumed that the refugees in the Central Asian states are ethnically the same as the host republic. Life expectancy for males is 47 years and for women 45 years.

Families form into clans and clans into tribes. Collectively the tribes form an ethnic group. All Afghan conflict is clan-based. The Hindu Kush and its adjoining mountains have ensured that no ethnic group ever completely dominated the country.

ALL AFGHAN CONFLICT IS CLAN-BASED.

The largest ethnic group are the Pashtun who account for 38

per cent of the Afghan population. Hence there are about 10 million Pashtuns, but there are 12 million Pashtuns in Pakistan. This ethnic group dominates almost half of Afghanistan but does not extend either to the northern or southern frontiers. Its capital is Kabul. It is followed by the Tajiks, with 25 per cent. They dominate in territory running south from Tajikistan, east of Herāt and in portions of the Afghan–Iranian border. The Hazaras, 19 per cent, are concentrated west of Kabul. They are treated as pariahs by the Pashtuns because they are Shiites. They tried to gain some autonomy in collaboration with the Northern Alliance. The Taliban punished them severely for this. The Baluchis occupy the southern part of the country. The Uzbeks (6 per cent) and the Turkmen border their states in Central Asia. There are other small ethnic groups, such as the Nuristani and Kyrgyz. About 84 per cent are Sunni Muslims and 15 per cent Shiites (Hazaras).

The country was laid waste during the civil war with the Soviet Union with many peasants fleeing to the cities or abroad. Agriculture survived in the north, in Tajik and Uzbek territory. The Taliban never succeeded in capturing the best land. Natural gas deposits, bordering on Central Asia, could not be developed during the incessant fighting of the last 25 years.

THE VAST MAJORITY OF THE POPULATION ARE EXTREMELY POOR AND FAMINE AND DISEASE HAVE BEEN CONSTANT COMPANIONS.

There is also copper, coal and other minerals. The vast majority of the population are extremely poor and famine and disease have been constant companions.

CENTRAL ASIA

To say that the people of Central Asia are miserably poor would be a statement of fact. To say that the region is rich would be an understatement: it is potentially fabulously rich. This is both good and bad news for everyone there. It guarantees that living standards will gradually rise but tension will also remain high as the ultimate prizes are so immense. Oil and gas are almost everywhere, and the largest deposits are in the biggest countries: Kazakhstan and Uzbekistan. Over a thousand types of valuable ores are to be found in Kazakhstan alone. Tajikistan has one of the world's largest deposits of uranium. It has also silver, gold, oil and natural gas. But what use are they as long as insecurity and strife plague the country? Unfortunately, it also means that the various clans and factions have something valuable to fight over.

KAZAKHSTAN

Regional policy within a developed state is very important. Its goal is to ensure that disparities between regions are reduced by state subsidies, for example. The richer regions provide subventions to the poorer. The gulf between Kazakhstan's regions is vast, ranging from the new oil rich in the south-west to the economic and ecological desolation of east and south Kazakhstan. In the course of the 1990s, the richer regions ensured that a redistribution of wealth in favour of the poorer regions did not take place. About half of

IN THE 1990S, THE RICHER REGIONS ENSURED THAT A REDISTRIBUTION OF WEALTH IN FAVOUR OF THE POORER REGIONS DID NOT TAKE PLACE.

current investment (most of it foreign) flows into the oil-rich south-west and the two capitals (Astana and Almaty) receive about a quarter. Almaty oblast and south Kazakhstan attract very little investment but are economically the least developed, are almost totally dependent on agriculture, are the most densely populated and have the lowest standard of living in the republic. Education and health care are almost absent. Not surprisingly, protests have been mounting since 1997. They are usually against the non-payment of wages and pensions but demands are being voiced for fundamental political and economic change. President Nazarbaev is not popular here. Reports that the Wahhabien (Islamic fundamentalists) are becoming more influential are appearing more often. In the north, the agricultural steppe and the industrial centres have suffered badly due to the downturn of the Kazakh and Russian economies. The coal and iron ore industries are in a bad state as industrial output dropped by a half during the 1990s. This has resulted in many Slavs emigrating. East Kazakhstan is an ecological disaster zone. It was the site of Soviet nuclear testing.

Since 1995 the oblasts have gained in influence and the President and government have lost influence. One reason for this is that the local presidential representative, the hakim, has sided more and more with the locals. Informal coalitions of hakims have formed to resist the implementation of unpopular central reforms. The centre does not invite nor wish the oblasts to have an input into decision making. This has led the oil-rich oblasts to band together. They have even considered setting up a sovereign oil republic which, in their own eyes, would be a second Kuwait.

The mining industry also has great potential. Kazakhstan is the world's leading producer of barytes, lead and wolfram. It is second in the world in production of chromate ore, silver and zinc and is third in the world for manganese. Its mineral reserves may top a trillion dollars. It has about 8 per cent of the world's reserves of iron ore. It is the sole producer of chromium in the northern hemisphere and has about 30 per cent of world deposits. The country has also about 25 per cent of the world deposits of uranium. The Tengiz oilfield may have up to 9 billion barrels (7 barrels = 1 tonne) of reserves and the Kashagan field, according to President Nazarbaev, may have six times the reserves of Tengiz.

The Slavs and Germans go, the Kazakhs stay

Kazakhstan is the only country in Central Asia where the population has declined since 1989. In 2001, the population was 14.8 million, over a million less than in 1989. This was in sharp contrast to Kazakhstan's neighbours. In Turkmenistan the population has increased by 34 per cent and in Uzbekistan by 17 per cent. Over the last decade about two million persons have left Kazakhstan, mainly Russians and Germans (800,000 to Germany). There is no danger of the Kazakhs dying out. Over the last decade their numbers have risen by 23 per cent. However the loss of so many Europeans, many of them possessing skills desperately needed in Kazakhstan, will slow economic development. This means that those joining the labour force are increasingly Kazakh. The age of the average Kazakh is now 20 years whereas the average Russian is 45 years old. One of the consequences of the decline of population is the rising ruralisation of the country. The numbers of those living in urban areas have declined and this has hit small towns hardest. Their numbers have halved over the last decade. This has led to a situation where the cities are still multi-ethnic but the countryside is almost entirely Kazakh.

Among the minorities, only the Europeans and the Tatars have declined. Dungans (Chinese Muslims) have risen by a quarter and Kurds by 30 per cent. Of concern to the Kazakhs was the rise of the Uzbek population, all concentrated on the Kazakh–Uzbek border. A thought was that Uzbekistan could use this minority to demand a redrawing of the border. One of the most interesting developments over the last decade has been the rapid rise of the illegal Chinese population. There may now be over 300,000 in Kazakhstan.

KYRGYZSTAN

The population is about 5 million, two thirds of whom are Kyrgyz. The percentage of Kyrgyz has been steadily increasing due to the emigration of over half a million Russians and Germans. As the Russians were mainly urban dwellers, the country is following the trend in Kazakhstan and Uzbekistan, ruralisation. Only about a third now live in towns. In contrast to Kazakhstan, Russians here have not formed nationalist political groups. They have simply left. Many of them were technically qualified and the country could ill afford to lose them. Education and health care budgets have

EDUCATION AND HEALTH CARE BUDGETS HAVE BEEN SLASHED AS SUBSIDIES FROM MOSCOW HAVE DISAPPEARED.

been slashed as subsidies from Moscow have disappeared. The country is split, east to west, by high mountain ranges (93 per cent of the country is mountainous) and this makes communications between north and south difficult.

Kyrgyzstan imports most of its oil and gas although it produces some. It produces a large surplus of hydroelectricity and exports it to China and other Central Asian states. Agriculture dominates its economy with stock grazing on the higher slopes and wheat and other crops in the valleys. After independence the country was cut off from its main Russian fertiliser and machinery supplies and did not have the resources to import them.

Gold, coal, uranium, antimony, mercury, tin, tungsten and polymetallic ores are all present. Gold now accounts for about a half of export earnings.

TAJIKISTAN

Given the civil war and parlous economic position of the country, it is surprising that the population increased during the 1990s and now stands at about 6.4 million. During the civil war of 1992–97 over 70,000 fled to Afghanistan but most have now returned. Over 600,000 sought refuge in other states and Russia and many are unlikely to return. Ethnic Russians used to dominate Dushanbe but there are only just over 100,000 left. The German minority, in the country since the 1880s, have almost all departed for Germany. The mountainous terrain means that about three quarters of the population live in the countryside. Rural poverty has driven over

300,000 into Dushanbe and its population is now over 1.1 million.

Education is severely underfunded and one child in five may not be attending school. Either they are needed for family work or their parents do not have clothes and shoes for them. Many dedicated teachers earn a pittance and have various other jobs to eke out a living. However, an educational élite is being educated. The Russian government funds a Slav university in Dushanbe. There is an Aga Khan university in Khorog, the capital of Badakhshan, in the east. There are seven Turkish secondary schools funded privately by Turks. The most able then move on to study in Turkey, along with others from Central Asia, on scholarships provided by the Turks.

Tajikistan has considerable mineral wealth but political instability prevents exploration and exploitation. Silver and gold are mined and some natural gas is produced. The country has the potential to become the largest exporter of hydro-electricity but at present it cannot meet its own energy needs.

In the Soviet Union, Tajikistan was the poorest of the republics. Almost half of its budget came from Moscow and cotton dominated the economy. Almost all of it was exported in return for grain and other food products. Severe drought during the last three years has hampered agricultural growth. Cotton production is one third of that of ten years ago. Food production

ONE IN SIX OF THE POPULATION WILL DIE OF HUNGER IF FOOD AID IS NOT PROVIDED.

about a half. One in six of the population will die of hunger if food aid is not provided.

Industry is dominated by the production of aluminium. However, there is no alumina in Tajikistan. It has to be imported from Ukraine, Kazakhstan and Azerbaijan. This was a classic example of Soviet planning. The goal was to make the various republics dependent on one another with Moscow pulling the strings. The smelter consumes almost half of the republic's energy and is a major pollutant of the environment. Its equipment is obsolete but it does bring in valuable foreign currency. It should be closed down but the government cannot afford to do this.

The war against the Taliban bodes well for Tajikistan. The civil war cost 60,000 lives and Tajikistan was spared the fate of Afghanistan by the peace agreement of 1997. The new industries are gun-running and heroin smuggling. Then there are the hordes of foreign journalists who have passed through, adding a tidy sum to the national GDP. The

THE NEW INDUSTRIES ARE GUN-RUNNING AND HEROIN SMUGGLING.

President has cleared all the gun-toting hoods off the streets of Dushanbe, a considerable feat. The country has found a new symbol to replace Lenin. He is Sumani, a tenth-century king – far enough back in history to prevent any conflict.

TURKMENISTAN

The population has grown spectacularly since 1989, the last census. The government claims that it is now over 5 million but the US Bureau of Census puts it at 4.5 million. Now over 60 per cent live in towns and this runs against the trend in other parts of Central Asia. Ruralisation is not overtaking the country. President Niyazov, Turkmenbashi, has attracted back over 300,000 ethnic Turkmen from other republics. Turkmen now make up over 80 per cent of the population and Turkmen is now the official language of communication. This has led many Russians to prepare to leave. They still make up about a third of the population of Ashgabat, the capital, and 11 per cent throughout the country. About 40 per cent of the population is under 14.

Given the rapidly growing child population, one might expect more and more resources to flow into education. The reverse is true. Thousands of teachers have been dismissed and school attendance reduced by a year to nine years. Classes of over forty are common and the children learn less and less. Those who want their children to go to a good school have to bribe their way in. Fifty dollars is normal but if it is a Turkish school this goes up to five hundred. Advanced education has collapsed. Less than one per cent of secondary school leavers go on to further study. Doctorates have been abolished. Getting in requires a sweetener of at least $12,000 but often more. University students in the west will be pleased to hear that local students may not be given low marks. This is having a dismal effect on standards. Bashi has clearly come to the conclusion that keeping the population ignorant is the best route to keeping them under control.

THOSE WHO WANT THEIR CHILDREN TO GO TO A GOOD SCHOOL HAVE TO BRIBE THEIR WAY IN.

The health service is in a parlous state. Local hospitals have been closed down, on direct orders from Bashi, and the ill must make their way to Ashgabat to seek treatment. It has to be paid for as well as all medicine. According to locals, infantile mortality is ten times as high as in western Europe. Dying children are sent home to die and, therefore, are not included in official statistics. Many Turkmen doctors and scientists have left, the Russians have returned to Russia and the Jews have emigrated to Israel and Germany.

DYING CHILDREN ARE SENT HOME TO DIE AND, THEREFORE, ARE NOT INCLUDED IN OFFICIAL STATISTICS.

If medical care for the population is declining, it is improving for Bashi. Siemens has built Bashi a state of the art heart clinic for $40 million with a special bed for him and beds for 25 others. In 1997, he underwent bypass surgery in Munich. Siemens arranged everything and the following year was permitted to open an office in Ashgabat. The German surgeon comes annually to check Bashi's health and never forgets to appear on Turkmen television to assure everyone that Bashi is in blooming health. Nor are Bashi's teeth forgotten. A Bavarian dentist flies in regularly to attend to the great man's mouth. Bashi wanted a modern neurological hospital. Siemens had to build it quickly but the contract was worth $27 million.

Daimler-Chrysler have also managed to enter the Bashi market. They have delivered a bullet-proof wagon which he drives personally. Each vice Prime Minister has a Mercedes 500 but ordinary ministers have to do with lesser Mercedes. However, the Germans do not have it all their own way. The

French and Turks are heavily involved in construction. Needless to say, no money is spared on the new edifices. Residents of the city may come home in the evening and find that their homes have disappeared. They have been demolished, on Bashi's orders, to make way for another glittering construction. Magnificent fountains and waterfalls decorate the capital, giving the impression that water is abundant. For the average citizen it is not. Water is cut off for several hours daily. True, water is free. So is gas but its supply is less erratic.

RESIDENTS OF THE CITY MAY COME HOME IN THE EVENING AND FIND THAT THEIR HOMES HAVE DISAPPEARED.

A rapidly growing industry is drugs. Turkmenistan is an important transit route from Afghanistan to Europe. This has had a disastrous effect on Turkmen youth. The number of addicts in Ashgabat has grown rapidly. Officially there are over 2,000 but unofficially there may be twenty times more. Over 2 per cent of those tested in a UN survey were found to be HIV positive. Turkmenistan does not have any drug treatment centres. Drug addicts are just put in jail.

TURKMENISTAN DOES NOT HAVE ANY DRUG TREATMENT CENTRES. DRUG ADDICTS ARE JUST PUT IN JAIL.

Bashi's dream is to be autarkic and thus not dependent on any outside state for anything. He has pushed grandiose schemes such as planting wheat and sugar beet in the Karakum desert. The beet did not appreciate the heat and withered away. Bashi's present dream is a massive man-made lake or reservoir in the Karakum to collect floodwater from the surrounding area. It is to cover 3,460 square km and to cost $6 billion. All irrigated land is to be connected to it. Bashi will not listen to specialists who point out that the water may evaporate before it gets to the lake. There is also the danger that Turkmenbashi lake could share the same fate as the Aral Sea. Speed is of the essence, the lake was to be constructed in ten years, now it is five years. The rise in the level of the Caspian Sea has led to flooding and the irrigation system is buckling under the strain of poor maintenance and pollution. Half of the irrigation water may be wasted at present.

Another Bashi dream is to build gas and oil pipelines to carry Turkmen hydrocarbons through Afghanistan to Pakistan and China. Turkmenistan has an 800 km border with Afghanistan. A proposed partner in this project is Iran with whom relations have been steadily improving over the last decade. There are now over 120 companies with Iranian involvement, and trade turnover with Iran more than trebled in the second half of the 1990s. Russia has put out feelers to Kazakhstan and Turkmenistan to build a pipeline through the two countries to Iran. President Putin visited Ashgabat during the summer of 2000 and signed contracts for the delivery of 30 billion cubic metres of gas to Russia. Moscow needs the gas to fulfil its contracts with western Europe. Turkmenistan has a lot of gas to sell. Claimed reserves are put at 11.1 trillion cubic metres, or about three times those of Russia's. A more realistic estimate would be 8 trillion cubic metres. Claimed oil reserves are 1 billion tonnes but a more accurate figure would be 700 million tonnes. Landlocked as it is, Turkmenistan needs the collaboration of competitors to get its gas to market. Output at present is only a quarter of

TURKMENISTAN NEEDS THE COLLABORATION OF COMPETITORS TO GET ITS GAS TO MARKET. that of 1989. The fall is due to the disruption in the wake of the collapse of the Soviet Union; the decision by Gazprom, the Russian gas monopoly, to stop carrying Turkmen gas to western European markets in 1994; and a dispute in 1997 over non-payment by Ukraine and the ongoing conflict with Gazprom. Things are now on a more even keel.

Earthquakes are a constant hazard in Turkmenistan. The latest was in December 2000 in the western part of the country. It damaged many buildings and ninety people may have died. Bashi denied all reports of an earthquake. Those affected, therefore, received no official aid and this led to demonstrations and portraits of Bashi being burnt.

UZBEKISTAN

Uzbekistan traditionally regards itself as the leading country in the region. Its population, just over 24 million, is by far the greatest. However, almost 850,000 emigrated during the 1990s. They were predominantly Russian and German. They felt that the country was becoming more Islamic and feared that there was no future for their children. As in Kazakhstan, the migrants included many skilled workers and technically qualified personnel. The Uzbek health service was badly hit as many Russian doctors left. Uzbeks will soon make up 80 per cent of the republic's population. As in Kazakhstan, the country is becoming increasingly rural. Almost two-thirds live in the countryside. Since families in rural areas are larger (on average about 7 members) than in the towns, the population is becoming younger. About 40 per cent are now under 16. This imposes huge pressures on the health and educational services which cannot cope. For political reasons, Uzbekistan has switched from the Cyrillic (Russian) to the Latin alphabet. This has compounded the difficulties facing an underfunded sector. Less than one in five go on to university education, a sharp drop from the one in three ten years ago. Standards in science and technology have declined as demand from Uzbek industry is modest. Previously Uzbeks enrolled in Russian universities and institutes and received high quality training in science and technology. This applies to all of Central Asia and is one of the high costs of independence.

THE YOUNG POPULATION IMPOSES HUGE PRESSURES ON THE HEALTH AND EDUCATIONAL SERVICES WHICH CANNOT COPE.

In 2000, there were proven oil reserves of over 600 million barrels but exploration has only just begun. There are huge proven reserves of natural gas. Uzbekistan has major deposits of gold and production, in 1999, was 80 tonnes. There are large deposits of silver, copper, lead, zinc, tungsten, coal and uranium.

A drawback for Uzbekistan is that the sources of its most important rivers, the Amu Darya and the Syr Darya, are outside its frontiers. The Amu Darya begins in Afghanistan and the Syr Darya in the Tien Shan mountains in China. These two rivers account for over 90 per cent of the water resources of Central Asia. Under the communists, huge dams were built upstream in Tajikistan and Kyrgyzstan (some of them left unfinished in 1991) to provide hydroelectric power and water for irrigation. The rest of the water flowed downstream to Uzbekistan, southern Kazakhstan and Turkmenistan. There was a strict system of quotas. Cotton production in Tajikistan and the fertile Fergana valley expanded rapidly under the communists. Rice output in Kazakhstan expanded almost thirty times. Unfortunately irrigation was very wasteful as concrete channels were not lined to prevent the seepage of water. Fertilisers and pesticides were heavily applied and rapidly polluted the land. Salinisation is now a major problem. As quantity was the main objective, the quality of long-staple cotton declined.

The rise in the population of the region has put greater pressure on water resources. Tajikistan and Kyrgyzstan, to augment their over-stretched budgets, have attempted to charge Kazakhstan and Uzbekistan for the water which flows downstream (free, of course, under the Soviets). This has caused increasing tension and Uzbekistan periodically cuts off gas supplies to Kyrgyzstan as a bargaining chip. However, the Fergana valley cannot do without the water. Kyrgyzstan does have a point. Under the Soviets it provided much of the water used for irrigation but only retained about a quarter of the water it collected every year. This led to a situation where half of the water used in southern Kazakhstan, Uzbekistan and Turkmenistan came from outside their republics. In the case of Turkmenistan, this reaches 98 per cent. A major problem during the Tajik civil war (1992–97) was the secur-

UZBEKISTAN PERIODICALLY CUTS OFF GAS SUPPLIES TO KYRGYZSTAN AS A BARGAINING CHIP.

ity of dams. The Unified Tajik Opposition threatened more than once to blow up the Usoi dam which holds back Lake Sarez's water. The lake is situated at an altitude of about 4,000 metres in the Bartang valley, in remote Gorno-Badakhshan region. If the Usoi dam collapsed it could endanger up to 5 million people in Tajikistan. It could also destroy large areas of the Fergana valley.

Security concerns were voiced again, in November 2001, during the US and Northern Alliance attacks against the Taliban in Afghanistan. Some feared that revenge attacks could wreak havoc as Tajikistan was supporting the fight against the Taliban.

> IF THE USOI DAM COLLAPSED IT COULD ENDANGER UP TO 5 MILLION PEOPLE IN TAJIKISTAN.

The major environmental problem in Uzbekistan is the Aral Sea area. At one time, it was the fourth largest lake in the world. It has lost over 60 per cent of its water and is now only just over half the area it was 40 years ago. Water usage has been traditionally wasteful and water costs are very low. President Karimov has been advised to increase the costs of water so as to conserve more but he adamantly refuses, fearing an explosion of protest. The region is now a health hazard. The once flourishing fishing industry is dead. Drinking water is polluted and this has increased infant mortality and reduced life expectancy to under 50 years of age.

> POLLUTED DRINKING WATER HAS INCREASED INFANT MORTALITY AND REDUCED LIFE EXPECTANCY TO UNDER 50 YEARS OF AGE.

The cotton crop failed in 1996 and 1998 and is nowhere near the government's target of 4 million tonnes a year. As cotton accounts for 40 per cent of export earnings and two thirds of hard currency earnings, it needs capital and know-how. Uzbekistan's goal is to become self-sufficient in grain but this has not been attained. Land has been switched from cotton to grain production but this is economically irrational because cotton income per hectare is up to three times that of grain. Cotton and gold prices have held up well since independence. This has helped cushion the economic transition and GDP per head may have dropped by about a quarter since 1992. This is about the same as in Kazakhstan. President Karimov's way of dealing with failed economic policies is to sack publicly a hakim or provincial governor. They are his appointees and are from the local clans.

THREE

ISLAM AND TERRORISM

AFGHANISTAN

Soviet forces invaded Afghanistan in December 1979 and turned what was an inter-clan, inter-tribe conflict into a jihad against the infidel. Few Russian scholars had a grasp of Islam outside their own frontiers. Hence they were in no position to warn the Kremlin about the consequences of its actions. Even had they been very prescient, the

> WHAT WAS AN INTER-CLAN, INTER-TRIBE CONFLICT INTO A JIHAD AGAINST THE INFIDEL.

aged communist leadership, headed by the drug-addicted Leonid Brezhnev, would not have listened. The documents reveal no inkling about the possible influence of Islam. They are all about the role of progressive social forces which are about to sweep away obscurantism and backwardness.

The United States began helping the anti-communist opposition before the Soviet intervention. However, Washington understood even less about Islam. It was only concerned about defeating the Soviets and driving them out of

Afghanistan. The sooner they were defeated and driven out of the country the better. That would represent a triumph for American policy. Once defeated in Afghanistan, Moscow could be undermined elsewhere. It was a purely military problem and should be solved by training and arming the opposition to the point where it could defeat comrade Ivan. Anyone who was willing to put his shoulder to the anti-communist wheel was welcome. Thousands flocked to Afghanistan but they were not motivated by anti-imperialism, they were driven by a religious duty to help fellow Muslims who were being oppressed by the infidel. The religious dimension was never taken into account by the west.

TALIBAN

The failure of the mujahidin to bring peace to Afghanistan after the Soviets left in 1989 opened the way for a movement which would do just that. The population was prepared to accept discipline if stability were guaranteed. There were many who had fought the Soviets and had become disillusioned with the never-ending fratricidal strife. They formed the fighting backbone. Then there were the young and idealistic looking for an organisation in which they could realise their ambitions to serve Allah and their fellow men. Many had received an education in the refugee camps in Pakistan. However, and most important of all, the movement found a charismatic leader, Mullah Mohammed Omar. An Islamic movement needs an influential spiritual leader. Omar knew how to lead and win converts. He was born near Kandahar into a poor, land-

MULLAH MOHAMMED OMAR KNEW HOW TO LEAD AND WIN CONVERTS.

less family. The Soviet invasion of 1979 interrupted his *madrasa* studies and he fought against the Najibullah regime between 1989 and 1992. He was wounded and lost the sight of the right eye. Married three times, he has five children, all studying in his *madrasa*. He became the ultimate authority and if one wanted something or a problem resolved he was consulted. He could instruct a commander to advance, order a governor to improve someone's lot and so on. He mediated between fractious commanders in order to help ordinary people. He did not ask for a reward, only that a just Islamic society should be promoted. By the end of 1994, about 12,000 young Afghani and Pakistani students had joined the Taliban. They then began to impose the strictest interpretation of the Sharia in the Muslim world. Girls' schools were closed and women were not to work outside the home. TV

> BY THE END OF 1994, ABOUT 12,000 YOUNG AFGHANI AND PAKISTANI STUDENTS HAD JOINED THE TALIBAN.

sets were smashed, music frowned upon and all males had to stop shaving and grow their beards long. Mullah Omar and his students set out for Kabul. Warlords scattered like chaff before them. It appeared they were terrified not of their weapons, which were modest, but of their spiritual power. Success breeds success and thousands of young men streamed to join the all-victorious movement. Many of these young men were quite happy within a wholly male environment. They had grown up as refugees in Pakistan and elsewhere without mothers, sisters or girl friends. Mullah Omar fraternal society was a home from home for them. It looked as if the Pashtuns – the Taliban was almost exclusively Pashtun – would again dominate Afghanistan from north to south and east to west.

However, there was one commander who was determined to resist the Taliban, Ahmad Shah Masoud. In February he confronted the Hazaras in southern Kabul and launched a murderous attack. They were driven out and struck a tactical alliance with the Taliban outside the city. In the extremely confused situation the Hazara leader Abdul Ali Mazari was killed. The Hazaras believed that he was thrown from a helicopter en route to imprisonment in Kandahar. Whatever the truth about Mazari's demise the episode permanently soured relations between the Hazaras and the Taliban. Masoud held on to Kabul. It was the first time that the Taliban had fought a major battle. It was also the first time they had been defeated. It did not deter them. Rather it made them even more determined to advance.

Herāt was under the control of Ishmael Khan. He had been an officer in the Afghan army when the Soviets invaded in December 1979. They thought that he and others in Herāt were accommodating but he and others launched a violent attack on the Soviets and the latter responded by destroying much of the city from the air. Over 20,000 died. Khan escaped to the countryside where his new guerrilla army took shape. Thousands of civilians fled to Iran. In 1995, as the ruler of Herāt, he had become unpopular and proved no match for the resurgent Taliban. They took the city in September and Khan fled to Iran.

Then came Mullah Omar's masterstroke. In Kandahar he wrapped and unwrapped the cloak of the Prophet around himself and was greeted with rapturous applause. He was proclaimed emir of Afghanistan. Even more important his

Muslim title afforded him leadership not only of Afghans but of all Muslims. A personal oath of allegiance was sworn to him. He proclaimed a jihad against President Rabbani's regime. There were to be no negotiations. It was now time

> **MULLAH OMAR'S MUSLIM TITLE AFFORDED HIM LEADERSHIP NOT ONLY OF AFGHANS BUT OF ALL MUSLIMS.**

for the end game. In September 1996 the Taliban roared into Kabul and the defenders scattered. Masoud managed to escape northwards with much of his armour. When the Taliban found Najibullah and his brother, they exacted a gruesome revenge. They were left hanging outside the presidential palace. After taking Kabul, the Taliban imposed their strict version of the Sharia. Girls' education ended – they were even banned from studying at home – and women driven out of administration. The Taliban carried on to Mazar-e Sharif and it appeared that the civil war would never end.

World interest in Afghanistan has waxed and waned. History has shown that the great powers, then the superpowers, ignored the country at their peril. This especially applies to the United States which was offered many opportunities after 1945 to play a leading role in its modernisation. They were all spurned. This policy was completely reversed after 11 September 2001.

> **THE UNITED STATES WAS OFFERED MANY OPPORTUNITIES TO PLAY A LEADING ROLE IN AFGHANISTAN'S MODERNISATION.**

Osama bin Laden and al-Qaeda

Osama bin Laden heeded the call to help fellow Muslims in Afghanistan in 1983. A member of a billionaire construction family in Saudi Arabia, the 26-year-old moved to a house outside Peshawar, Pakistan. It was a meeting point for Arabs wanting to fight the communist invaders. He fought against the Soviets from 1984–1989. Al-Qaeda was founded in Jaji, Afghanistan, in 1989. A formative influence on Osama bin Laden's thinking was Abdullah Azzam, a Palestinian. He had taught Islamic studies at Jeddah university and Osama was one of his students. They met up again in Peshawar. Azzam argued that the jihad and the gun were the only weapons. Do not bother with conferences, meetings or dialogue. Afghanistan was the first step on the road to world liberation. Every Muslim is duty bound to join the armed struggle because a jihad had been declared against the Soviet invaders. Also present in Peshawar was the head of a mosque in Karachi, Pakistan, Mohammed Omar. Bin Laden invested money in Omar's mosque and bought him a house. During the 1980s, bin Laden and Omar visited mosques in Saudi Arabia and other Arab countries, encouraging young Arabs to fight with the Afghan mujahidin and instructing them on how to get there. The house in Peshawar became the centre for recruitment in 35 countries, including all Arab countries, the US, Britain, France, Germany and throughout Scandinavia. They could do this because they were allies in the battle against Soviet communism. Bin Laden bankrolled the whole operation.

THE JIHAD AND THE GUN WERE THE ONLY WEAPONS. DO NOT BOTHER WITH CONFERENCES, MEETINGS OR DIALOGUE.

One of the reasons for setting up al-Qaeda was that bin Laden became more and more concerned about Arab governments infiltrating the mujahidin to identify those who might eventually oppose them. A more secure organisation was needed and thus al-Qaeda came into being. Only those who had been vetted carefully now gained access to the house in Peshawar. Some 30,000 Arabs fought with the mujahidin, according to some sources. They were greatly aided by the $2 billion provided for the mujahidin by the Americans and the Saudis. There was also the point that there was a 75 per cent discount on flights from Riyadh to Peshawar.

Taking part in a jihad was a formative experience for those involved. Afghanistan was the place where all Arab and Muslim resistance groups met up, shared experience and acquired new skills. With the Soviets defeated, the Arabs returned home. Their governments had every reason to be wary of their religious zeal and military expertise. They joined radical Islamic groups in Algeria and Egypt. They were bloodily suppressed. The survivors looked again to bin Laden who had returned to Saudi Arabia, in 1990. When Saddam Hussein invaded Kuwait, bin Laden offered his warriors to the Saudi royal family. They would defend the state against the Iraqis, if they attacked. His offer was rejected and soon the holy ground of Mecca and Medina was resounding to the heavy presence of the US and its allies. Bin Laden and his militants had found a new mission. Rid Saudi Arabia of US troops on behalf of Muslims

AFGHANISTAN WAS WHERE ALL ARAB AND MUSLIM RESISTANCE GROUPS MET UP, SHARED EXPERIENCE AND ACQUIRED NEW SKILLS.

throughout the world. The sharia was to be implemented worldwide and the enemies of Islam fought wherever they were. Hence al-Qaeda became an international organisation, headed by bin Laden. The jihad against the Soviets was now extended into a world jihad. Many who had fought in Afghanistan flocked to the cause and they were joined by younger men. Soon there were representatives from about 50 countries.

THE SHARIA WAS TO BE IMPLEMENTED WORLDWIDE AND THE ENEMIES OF ISLAM FOUGHT WHEREVER THEY WERE.

In 1991, bin Laden was disowned by his family and his country. He had to go and he moved to Khartoum, Sudan. He was especially welcome there as a military coup, in 1989, had brought to power a *mélange* of military and religious leaders. They welcomed militant Islamic groups, offering them military training and the opportunity to plan the worldwide Islamic revolution. Al-Qaeda set up an international financial system, charity organisations, legitimate businesses and many illegal undertakings, from card fraud to bank robberies. Al-Qaeda became a global organisation.

AL-QAEDA SET UP AN INTERNATIONAL FINANCIAL SYSTEM, CHARITY ORGANISATIONS, LEGITIMATE BUSINESSES AND MANY ILLEGAL UNDERTAKINGS.

It became influential because other Islamic movements were willing to join it. A key recruit was Egypt's Islamic Jihad. It was headed by Ayman al-Zawahari, a surgeon from a rich family in Alexandria, sometimes known as the doctor or the professor. He had fought in Afghanistan. Islamic Jihad was responsible for the murder of President Anwar Sadat, in 1981, because he had made peace with Israel. Al-Zawahari became bin Laden's personal physician. The two movements merged in 1998 and al-Zawahari became number two to bin Laden. Two top Jihad militants took over pivotal positions in al-Qaeda: Mohammad Atef and Abu Ubaidah al-Banshiri. They became respectively head of terrorist training and financial affairs. Atef was killed by an American bomb in Afghanistan in November 2001.

During the 1990s, Jihad had established a network of charities, fraudulent businesses and safe houses throughout the Balkans, the Middle East and Azerbaijan. Bin Laden's supporters had extensive links with Algerians in France and Algerians and Moroccans in Spain. They were also well represented in Italy, Germany, France and Britain. Bin Laden was obliged to leave Khartoum in 1996 and move to Kwost, Afghanistan. In 1988, Sudanese intelligence approached Washington offering to provide detailed information on al-Qaeda and its leaders. Perhaps an American official could visit Khartoum to be briefed. The Clinton administration just ignored the invitation. This must rank as a major intelligence blunder by the CIA.

The bombings of the US embassies in Kenya and Tanzania, in August 1998, the attack on USS *Cole*, in 2000, and the 11

IN 1988, SUDANESE INTELLIGENCE APPROACHED WASHINGTON OFFERING TO PROVIDE DETAILED INFORMATION ON AL-QAEDA. THE CLINTON ADMINISTRATION JUST IGNORED THE INVITATION.

September 2001 attack on the World Trade Center, were all

planned from his new base. The offensive against US interests followed the declaration of war against the United States in a fatwa in August 1996. As many as 70,000 fighters may have been trained in al-Qaeda camps.

The leadership of al-Qaeda is mainly Saudi. Much of the funding comes from the kingdom of Saudi Arabia. It may seem incongruous that a royal family permits the funding of an international terrorist organisation. After all, one of its targets is the house of Saudi itself. The explanation appears to be that the royal family believes that it is buying protection from attack. To add to a complex situation, Wahhabism is the official Islamic doctrine in Saudi Arabia. But this purified form of Islam has followers who engage in violence in the Caucasus and Central Asia.

Those who become holy warriors are profoundly alienated from the western world. Some come from open societies, such as Britain, where they have received a secular education. However, they have also been formed by an Islamic education and this has obliterated western, secular values. The major casualty

THESE HOLY WARRIORS REGARD TOLERANCE AS A WEAKNESS WHICH PROMOTES ERROR.

is tolerance. These Muslims regard tolerance as a weakness which promotes error.

Possibly the most influential form of religious education among Muslims is that of the Deobandi movement. The original *madrasa* is near New Delhi. India has over 15,000 *madrasas* and Pakistan 4,000. Millions now study in south and south-east Asia. Some claim that the movement's teachings have heavily influenced the Taliban. Among the objectives of the Deobandi schools are the purification of Islam from the accretions of the past two centuries and a return to the teaching of the Qur'an and precedents set by Muhammad or his early followers (Hadith). It rejects the world of politics and has formed its own communities. Stu-

> AMONG THE OBJECTIVES OF THE DEOBANDI SCHOOLS ARE THE PURIFICATION OF ISLAM . . . AND A RETURN TO THE TEACHING OF THE QUR'AN.

dents may not read newspapers or watch television. Western science is rejected as un-Islamic. However mathematics is on the curriculum. Students can remain twenty years in a *madrasa* and then go off and set up their own school. There are many *madrasas* along the border with Afghanistan, dominated by Pashtun (the Taliban is 90 per cent Pashtun). Many of the Taliban leaders were educated here as refugees in the 1980s. The Pakistani government plans to found new *madrasas* which will include computing science and English as part of the curriculum. Most of Pakistan's *madrasas* teach a formal version of Islam which emphasises correct behaviour. Hence it is not surprising that the Taliban focuses so much on regulating social life. This involves the banning of music, television and kite-flying. Also the growing of beards, the wearing of the burka, the removal of women from education and work outside the home are natural part of the new order. A logical extension of this is intolerance towards foreign cultures and the symbols of other religions such as the Buddhist statues in Bamiyan which were demolished in 2000. One can argue that the extreme cruelty and intolerance practised by the Taliban are aberrations from the teachings of the Deobandi movement. Nevertheless the Taliban won many adherents as did the al-Qaeda movement. It is this strand which has influenced the thinking of the Tajik Renaissance Party and the Islamic Movement of Uzbekistan.

ISLAM AND VIOLENCE

There are 1.2 billion Muslims and Islam is the fastest-growing world religion. If the events of 11 September 2001 represent the true face, how does one explain this? The answer is that the slaughter of the innocents on that black day is not the true face of Islam.

The term Islam means submission and is related to the Arab word salām (peace). When the prophet Muhammad provided Arabs with his divine inspirations he regarded, as part of his mission, the ending of the murderous conflicts and feuds which were commonplace in the Middle East. He survived several assassination attempts and violence had to be used to survive. Hence the Qur'an was written amid an orgy of violence but attempted to find a way out of the strife and to promote a peaceful lifestyle. There are passages which appear violent. Muslims, after a battle, were to 'kill everyone where they could be found'. However there are passages which offer clemency. Therefore, 'if they let you live, if they do not declare war against you, and they offer you peace, God does not permit you to harm them'. According to the Qur'an, the only justifiable war is a war of self-defence. Muslims 'may not initiate hostilities'. Whereas the Old Testament speaks of an eye for an eye, a tooth for a tooth, the Qur'an suggests that there is virtue in not exacting revenge. The jihad is not one of the five pillars of Islam (confessing the faith; prayer;

ACCORDING TO THE QUR'AN, THE ONLY JUSTIFIABLE WAR IS A WAR OF SELF-DEFENCE.

fasting; giving of alms; pilgrimage to Mecca) but, it should be added, some Muslims do add jihad as the sixth pillar. The word means struggle; a struggle to put into practice God's will in all its aspects; personal, economic, social and political. Those who regard jihad as armed struggle, perceive Islam to be under threat from secular forces. The latter's

JIHAD MEANS STRUGGLE; A STRUGGLE TO PUT INTO PRACTICE GOD'S WILL IN ALL ITS ASPECTS.

goal is the extirpation of Islam. Hence the jihad is to defend Islam against modernisation and globalisation.

However, Islamic teaching is not only derived from the Qur'an but also from the hadith or the collection of traditions recording the words and deeds of Muhammad. These traditions are second only to the Qur'an in providing the Muslim faithful with many of the detailed instructions for their religious practice and daily life, based on the pattern of Muhammad's own life. Where the Qur'an and traditions do not provide guidance on a particular subject, rules are derived by consensus of the religious leaders (ijma) and by analogous reasoning (qiyas). The combination of the Qur'an, hadith, ijma and qiyas have been used by Islamic scholars to create the immensely detailed body of rules and regulations known as the Sharia, or Islamic law.

The Sharia regulates every aspect of a Muslim's devotional

and personal life, but also the governing of an Islamic state. Compiled at a time when Islam was in the ascendancy politically and militarily, the Sharia assumes that political power rests with the conquering Muslims. There are many rules relating to non-Muslims but they are considered second-class citizens. They must adhere to a number of restrictions designed to reinforce their second-class status. Another feature of the Sharia are the severe punishments for certain crimes, such as amputation for theft, stoning for adultery, and so on. Any Muslim who converts to another religion can be considered to have committed state treason. As such the apostate must be killed. The Sharia considers women to be of less value than Muslim men, and this is reflected in many rules concerning inheritance, compensation, legal testimony, and so on. They are restricted by numerous rules ensuring their modesty and preventing them from leading men astray. Many scholars consider that the Sharia was quite moderate and lenient according to the standards of the day when it came into being in the eighth and ninth centuries. It has remained unchanged since then. This means that, according to modern western norms, it appears extremely harsh. The strict sanctions against those who deviate from the existing rules has ensured that the Sharia has survived unchanged for eleven centuries. The debate about whether and how much it can be changed began in the nineteenth century. However, the rise of radical Islam, in the middle of the twentieth century, and which continues in the twenty-first, has made it very difficult

> **UNDER SHARIA LAW, NON-MUSLIMS MUST ADHERE TO A NUMBER OF RESTRICTIONS DESIGNED TO REINFORCE THEIR SECOND-CLASS STATUS.**

to debate the modernisation of Islam. Those who do face many risks and this includes assassination. No Islamic country is ruled according to the full Sharia. However, many contain parts of it within their legislation. For example, the rule that apostates from Islam should be executed is part of the state law of Saudi Arabia, Iran, Sudan, to name only a few. Even when the Sharia is not legally enforced, the prevailing culture leads to discrimination against minorities. The ultimate goal of Muslim radicals is to introduce the full Sharia as widely as possible in the world, and thus create an Islamic state similar to that in Medina in Muhammad's time.

THE ULTIMATE GOAL OF MUSLIM RADICALS IS TO INTRODUCE THE FULL SHARIA AS WIDELY AS POSSIBLE IN THE WORLD.

In the light of the above the Taliban were acting within the Sharia. Their spiritual leader, Mullah Omar, interpreted the law and provided spiritual and legal guidance. Infidels and apostates can be killed. Hence the al-Qaeda organisation, in practising terror, could claim to be acting according to the Sharia. Their fighters were trained in Afghan camps and swore to be loyal to their leaders. This included laying down their life when necessary. A Muslim practises his faith but at death is not certain to gain access to paradise. Holy warriors, those who die during a jihad, enter paradise as a reward for their sacrifice. In late November 2001, several hundred al-Qaeda fighters, staged a revolt in a fortress outside Mazar-i Sharif, where they were being held prisoner. They fought until the last

HOLY WARRIORS, THOSE WHO DIE DURING A JIHAD, ENTER PARADISE AS A REWARD FOR THEIR SACRIFICE.

man was dead. They did not wish to live as prisoners but to die as holy martyrs.

The goal of Islamic radicals is revolution or replacing those now in power. There are three main reasons for using terror as a tactic. In the earlier stages of the conflict it can radicalise the masses. It provokes those who are attacked to respond in kind, whether they are the security forces or rival terrorists. During the acute phase of the revolutionary struggle, it wears down the will of the existing power elites. After the revolution, it imposes harsher discipline on the masses. They have to be purified of the bad habits they have picked up during the previous regime. It is a basic tenet of belief that returning to the fundamentals of the faith strengthens society. The nearer society approaches purity the more successful it becomes. The radicals believe that nothing in the infidel world can stop them from being victorious. Al-Qaeda has cells in over 50 countries. Their task is to carry out missions which will begin the first stage of the revolutionary struggle. The struggle will continue until final victory is achieved or when the cell has been wiped out. Others will then form a new cell and continue the battle. The more successful the terror cells become the more adherents the cause will attract. Success breeds success. The defeat suffered by Islamic countries in their great confrontation with the west in the nineteenth century need not be final.

THE MORE SUCCESSFUL THE TERROR CELLS BECOME THE MORE ADHERENTS THE CAUSE WILL ATTRACT. SUCCESS BREEDS SUCCESS.

Every radical believes the clock of time can be wound backwards.

The Taliban and al-Qaeda have lost, for now.

CENTRAL ASIA

Russia came to Islam; Islam did not come to Russia. As the empire expanded so the number of Muslims grew. The Caucasus (except Armenia and Georgia) and Central Asia were overwhelmingly Muslim. The Tatars and Bashkirs, to be found along the Volga, were also Muslims. Islam quickly assumed the role of being the second most important faith in Russia, after Russian Orthodoxy. The communists inherited about 20 million Muslims: 17 million Sunnis and 3 million Shiites. In 1949, the communist party estimated there were 30 million. In the 1989 Soviet census there were 54 million citizens belonging to Muslim nationalities. Had the Soviet Union not collapsed in 1991, Muslims would have made up a majority of the population of the Soviet Union at some point in the twenty-first century.

In 1917 there had been about 20,000 mosques. By 1929 only 4,000 were still open. Their numbers continued to decline so that, for example, in Kyrgyzstan, in 1941, there was only one functioning prayer house. Stalin, in order to attract more support for the war effort, liberalised religious policy in 1943. Mosques and prayer houses were then opened and registered. Numbers of mosques increased to 416 in 1949. The anti-religious policies of Stalin, after 1947, and Khrushchev, 1958-64, reduced the numbers to 309 in 1964. Half of the mosques were traditionally in the

IN KYRGYZSTAN, IN 1941, THERE WAS ONLY ONE FUNCTIONING PRAYER HOUSE.

Russian Federation. The Stalin persecution focused mainly on Tajikistan and Uzbekistan. In the latter republic, in 1953, most of the functioning mosques were in Tashkent and Tashkent oblast. Whole areas had no mosques at all. The same was true of Kazakhstan and Turkmenistan. This meant that huge swathes of territory were not served by a mosque or prayer house.

The number of believers is difficult to gauge. It is striking that the number of mosques, in 1949, was considerably fewer than the number of Lutheran churches. Old Believers, Baptists and Roman Catholics also had more places of worship. However, the number of Muslim clergy continued to mount, often in inverse proportion to the number of mosques. In 1970, there were 543 clergy but, in 1985, 1,540. Only a small part of these had received higher religious education. In general, the level of religious expertise was modest. Yet the number of unregistered clergy greatly exceeded the registered. This was especially true of Central Asia. In general, over time, mosque attendance dropped, but attendance at Islamic festivals increased. In the Soviet Union, in the 1960s, attendance at festivals was around half a million while 150,000 attended mosque on Fridays. About three quarters of them were male.

Islam, unlike the other religions, did not have one centre but four. The Directorate of the Muslims of Central Asia was in Tashkent; of European Russia and Siberia, in Ufa, Bashkortostan; of the North Caucasus in Buinaksk, Dagestan; and of Transcaucasus in Baku, Azerbaijan. The lack of unity was underlined by the fact that each used a different language.

Arabic was only used in Buinaksk. Hence there was consider-able autonomy and this was underlined by the quite different practices employed in the four regions.

The sermon is an integral part of the Friday and festival prayer service. The clergy had to tread a fine line between loyalty to the Soviet regime and being true to their religion. Usually they maintained that there was no contradiction between the teachings of the Qur'an and communism. Indeed, Allah was using Marx and Engels to lead the faithful to socialism and communism. Many preachers averred that all social progress achieved in the Soviet Union was nothing else but the im-plementation of the teachings of the Qur'an. However, the

ALLAH WAS USING MARX AND ENGELS TO LEAD THE FAITHFUL TO SOCIALISM AND COMMUNISM.

clergy conformed and did not preach religion. On the other hand, they stressed the precepts of a moral life and prayer and in so doing enhanced their influence.

The activities of unregistered Muslim associations, over time, vastly exceeded those of official Islam. Parallel Islam expanded to meet the needs of believers. One Russian scholar, researching Central Asia from the 1960s onwards, estimated that registered mosques and religious societies, official Islam, only accounted for 1 per cent of all religious activity. Parallel Islam, therefore, supplied the other 99 per cent. The latter, of course, was very difficult for the authorities to monitor. A major reason for this was that parallel Islam had to operate clandestinely. Groups were small and operated unobtrusively. Most of them operated at cemeteries.

At a conference in Tashkent, in 1968, communist officials expressed their frustration at the difficulties they faced in dealing with Islam. One pointed out that in Kyrgyzstan there were ten unofficial mosques for every registered one. The same proportion applied to the clergy. The parallel clergy were usually sons of mullahs as it was the Central Asian tradition for the calling to remain within certain families. There were also underground religious schools (*madrasas*) for adults and children. Nevertheless the large majority of parallel clergy were pensioners. As soon as unregistered mosques and religious establishments were closed down even more sprang up. A raft of new legislation was introduced, but had little effect. In the 1980s, hundreds of unofficial mosques were 'exposed' and found to have been operating for years. Often they were disguised as tea houses on collective farm land. After an initial expression of official horror everything reverted to normal.

IN THE 1980S, HUNDREDS OF UNOFFICIAL MOSQUES WERE 'EXPOSED' AND FOUND TO HAVE BEEN OPERATING FOR YEARS . . . DISGUISED AS TEA HOUSES.

Over time the parallel clergy became bolder in their criticisms of the official clergy and even called for defiance of Soviet law. The most outspoken were in the Fergana valley and Tajikistan. By the 1980s they were calling on believers to boycott registered mosques and not to buy meat and other products in state stores because they were 'unclean'. In Tajikistan some stated that it was forbidden to bury Soviet soldiers who had died in Afghanistan because they had fought against 'true Muslims'.

In Tajikistan and Uzbekistan, during the 1970s and 1980s, an increasing number of mullahs were arrested and put on trial for teaching the Qur'an. The practice appears to have spread because of the perceived lack of understanding by youth of Islam. The main subjects were Arabic and the Qur'an. In Tajikistan a group led by Said Abdullo Nuri was the precursor of that republic's Islamic Renaissance Party. In Uzbekistan, Muhammad Rustamov and Abduwali Mirzaev and their followers opened schools (*madrasas*) for small groups of children in many parts of the Fergana valley. The material included the works of leading Islamic activists from other parts of the Islamic world. These men had radicalised and politicised Islam in Egypt and Pakistan. These developments appear to have been influenced by the revolution in Iran. In 1982, in Tajikistan, as many as 21 schools teaching children and adults were 'discovered' by the authorities. More of these came to light the following year.

The Wahhabi movement in Tajikistan appears to have been founded in the early 1980s by young unregistered clerics. The name goes back to an eighteenth-century trend in Saudi Arabia which had attempted to go back to 'authentic' Islam. The clerics expressed support for the Khomeini government in Iran and had material confiscated which was anti-Soviet and anti-communist. The Soviet authorities then began using the term Wahhabi to describe all who opposed official Islam. In many cases they had no connection with this strand of Islam and certainly no links with Saudi Arabia. A factor in the growing politicisation of Islam was the Soviet invasion of Afghanistan in December 1979. In 1983, the Jemiat-e Islam, the Islamic political organisation which led the resistance to the Marxist government in Afghanistan, claimed to have 2,500 followers in Tajikistan. If true, this was political dynamite.

The communists also did battle with the religious faith healers. Not surprisingly, as official medical services were inadequate, more and more people began turning to them. Even communists and government functionaries were among their patients. Despite the fact that some of their patients ended up in hospital as a result of their efforts to heal them, where they usually died, their popularity did not decline. Another growing practice were religious chain letters. Those who copied them for distribution were promised success in life. This attracted many schoolchildren. The Qur'an and cassettes of prayers were sold illegally in large numbers. Pilgrimages to holy places became more and more popular in Central Asia, especially in Tajikistan.

Central Asia has a long tradition of non-conformist Islam. Impetus was provided by the religious establishment working closely with the ruling khans. Opposition groups formed into Sufi tariqas (orders). These split and senior figures, or ishans, founded their own order. They preached asceticism, abstinence and meditation. This was designed to bring followers closer to Allah. Those who joined an order promised to be faithful to the ishan to whom they handed over part of their income. The ishans could also play an important political role. Many of them

THOSE WHO JOINED AN ORDER PROMISED TO BE FAITHFUL TO THE ISHAN TO WHOM THEY HANDED OVER PART OF THEIR INCOME.

were involved in the Basmachi movement against the communists and could deploy extreme violence.

Ishans could have up to 500 followers and even a thousand. They were particularly widespread in southern Kazakhstan, Uzbekistan and Tajikistan. When an ishan in Samarkand oblast died in 1969, over 3,000 attended his funeral from all over Uzbekistan. His tomb became a place of pilgrimage. Some ishans encouraged young men to refuse to serve in the Soviet Army and young people to avoid the communist Pioneers and Komsomol. Usually believers did not confront the Soviet regime. If a mosque were 'discovered', the authorities ordered its demolition. Instead of protesting, they pulled it down and immediately began building another one nearby. A communist official, in the 1980s, lamented that Muslims paid lip service to the regime but did as they pleased.

Clerics attempted to 'modernise' Islam by relegating some practices to the background. They explained, in modern language, the advantages of fasting, for example. Islam was to be seen as a progressive religion which addressed

CLERICS ATTEMPTED TO 'MODERNISE' ISLAM BY RELEGATING SOME PRACTICES TO THE BACKGROUND.

the real problem of the world. This was of great importance in ensuring the survival of Islam as most believers were male pensioners. This was in direct contrast to the Russian Orthodox Church which was mainly attended by women pensioners. Natural disasters led to greater observance of religion. There was a major revival of religious activity in Tashkent after the devastating earthquake of 1966. Floods in Karakalpak autonomous republic, in 1969, had the same effect.

Islam gave up open opposition to the Soviet regime in the 1930s. Afterwards it adapted and sought ways of stressing Muslim identity. Muslims were different. The difference between republics was stressed and this led to growing nationalism which surfaced in dramatic form under Gorbachev. In 1986, the new Soviet leader had only harsh words for Islam in a speech in Tashkent which was not published at the time. This changed dramatically in 1989, in the aftermath of the 1988 millennium celebrations of the Russian Orthodox Church. Islam was now attributed a positive role and regarded as a partner in the struggle against alcoholism, crime and drugs. Large numbers of mosques were reopened and a religious journal in Uzbek, which provided elementary information about Islam, began publication. The existing Soviet order for the control of Islam was breaking down. A mass demonstration in Tashkent, in February 1989, against the incumbent, Soviet-appointed mufti, saw him depart and replaced by one acceptable to local believers. Each republic sought to establish its own independent organisations. In 1990 the first legal Islamic party for decades emerged, the Islamic Renaissance Party. Its goals were to revitalise Islam and to represent and promote the interests of Soviet Muslims.

> ISLAM WAS NOW ATTRIBUTED A POSITIVE ROLE AND REGARDED AS A PARTNER IN THE STRUGGLE AGAINST ALCOHOLISM, CRIME AND DRUGS.

POST-COMMUNISM OR RETURN TO THE PAST

The new rulers of the Central Asian states sought to identify with Islam but also to keep it under control. For instance, Islam Karimov, when taking the oath of office as President of Uzbekistan, did so with one hand on the Qur'an and the other on the constitution. In 1989–90, President Gorbachev justified harsh measures by pointing to 'Islamic fundamentalism'. There were mass disturbances throughout Central Asia, and Moscow always underlined the presence of portraits of Ayatollah Khomenei and the 'green flag of Islam' in its statements. President Rakhmonov, of Tajikistan, claimed, in 1993, that the civil war was between 'obscurantism, represented by Islamic fundamentalism, and the concept of progress and the democratic development of society'. The latter, of course, were represented by the communist forces which he headed. President Karimov used the example of Tajikistan as a warning about giving Islam a free rein in the republic. This had led to anarchy and civil war and therefore Islamic groups, particularly in the Fergana valley, had to be suppressed. Many new mosques were opened with aid from Saudi Arabia, Turkey and other Muslim countries. Educational establishments, including universities, appeared, again with financial help from abroad. Muslim clerics came to preach and to invite students to study abroad. This alarmed the secular rulers and they quickly attempted to develop controls akin to those of the Soviet period. Islam was officially an integral part of the national cultural heritage but had to be carefully monitored and guided into the correct channels. In other words, fundamentalists must not be permitted to politicise Islam. The Soviets devoted much energy and considerable resources in an attempt to 'tame' Islam and make it a private affair which did not spill over into everyday life. They failed and Islam by 1991 was more dynamic than several decades earlier. This is the world the new states have inherited. The evidence so far is that most Muslims are moderate but that there are regions such as the Fergana valley, and also Tajikistan, where adherents want a more Islamic way of life and are not satisfied with secular authorities.

ISLAM BY 1991 WAS MORE DYNAMIC THAN SEVERAL DECADES EARLIER.

ISLAMIC TERRORISTS OR DRUG SMUGGLERS?

Central Asia was shocked by the conflict between the Islamic Movement of Uzbekistan (IMU) and the armed forces of Tajikistan, Kyrgyzstan and Uzbekistan in the summer and autumn of 1999. The conflict resumed in August 2000. It transpired that the national armed forces were in very poor shape and in no condition to destroy the insurgents. The countries involved argued that the incursions from Afghanistan of Muslim fundamentalist fighters were also a threat to international security. The UN and Organisation for Security and Cooperation in Europe duly expressed concern. Russia talked of uniting the Commonwealth of Independent States (CIS) in the struggle against international terrorism and of promoting a global coalition against this new, deadly threat. Russia linked the events in Central Asia to the ongoing war in Chechnya which it regarded as a war against international terrorism, as foreigners were fighting with the Chechens. To keep matters in perspective,

Uzbek troops never engaged at any one time more than a hundred insurgents. Instead of international terrorism some analysts saw the conflict as one over drug routes to Russia and the west. Over 70 per cent of Afghan drug production (7 million tonnes in 2000) passes through Central Asia.

SOME ANALYSTS SAW THE CONFLICT AS ONE OVER DRUG ROUTES TO RUSSIA AND THE WEST.

THE BATTLE OF BATKEN

Insurgents from Tajikistan began penetrating the isolated south-west part of Kyrgyzstan, part of the Fergana valley, in July 1999. They were identified as Uzbek refugees who, from 1997 onwards, had been forced out of the Fergana valley in Uzbekistan because they had been labelled religious extremists. As a result they had fled to Tajikistan and Afghanistan. They were regarded as part of the IMU. They had a base in Tajikistan and their assumed goal was to enter Uzbekistan over the unguarded Kyrgyz–Uzbek border at Batken. Once in Uzbekistan they would attempt to overthrow the Karimov regime and proclaim an Islamic republic.

On 16 August the Uzbek air force bombed villages in Tajikistan and also in Kyrgyzstan. Four Kyrgyz civilians were killed in the attack. Uzbekistan had not received clearance from the other two states for the attacks. It thought it had the right to take unilateral action. The insurgents, at the end of August, again crossed into Kyrgyzstan from Tajikistan and took a Kyrgyz general and four Japanese geologists hostage. The Uzbeks again bombed the border area. President Akaev sacked his minister of defence for failing completely to deal with the insurgents. Uzbekistan sharply criticised Tajikistan for permitting armed bands to use its territory and Kyrgyzstan for being incapable of dealing with the insurgents. So desperate did President Akaev become that he mobilised not only his army but paramilitary forces as well. These consisted of sportsmen, mountaineers and anyone who would fight. They were promised double pay and some other privileges. After the operation the military refused to pay them the agreed sum and deducted from it the cost of uniforms worn during fighting. They only obtained redress after organising a protest demonstration. During the operation soldiers were advised to fire as few rounds as possible as the state was short of money to buy replacements.

SOLDIERS WERE ADVISED TO FIRE AS FEW ROUNDS AS POSSIBLE AS THE STATE WAS SHORT OF MONEY TO BUY REPLACEMENTS.

The foreign ministers of Kazakhstan, Kyrgyzstan, Tajikistan and Uzbekistan met in Osh, Kyrgyzstan, to deal with the problem. Since there were many nationalities among the in-surgents, they classified their conflict with them as a struggle against international terrorism. This caused more problems. Moscow and Dushanbe identified the terrorists as part of the Uzbek opposition. Uzbekistan saw them as part of the former united Tajik opposition. The Central Asian and Russian press linked the insurgents to the conflict in Dagestan and Chechnya. The mastermind pulling all the strings was Osama bin Laden. The conflict continued until late October

THE MASTERMIND PULLING ALL THE STRINGS WAS OSAMA BIN LADEN.

when the Japanese geologists were freed. Tokyo denied it had paid a ransom but local sources claimed that big money had been involved. The terrorists returned to their base in Tajikistan. The battle of Batken had cost 32 Kyrgyz their lives. A Kyrgyz security official estimated that there were up to 5,000 rebels in camps along the border waiting for an opportunity to cross again into Tajikistan. These men had links to the Taliban. Their leader had been Djuma Namangani, an Uzbek, who was a Taliban commander in Afghanistan.

The insurgents appear to have been former members of the UTO. When it was integrated into the Tajik armed forces after the peace agreement of 1997 the Tajiks were not keen to accept Uzbeks and other nationalities. They became free agents and the Tajik authorities were quite incapable of dealing with them. The Kyrgyz government took it for granted that the insurgents would return. They began desperate efforts to fortify the border and set up 64 new border posts. This was not the first time that bloody conflict had visited Batken. In 1989 there had been confrontations between Tajik collective farmers and Kyrgyz after the Tajiks had occupied 200 ha of Kyrgyz land. Later Batken became known as 'little Colombia' because of drug dealing.

BATKEN BECAME KNOWN AS 'LITTLE COLOMBIA' BECAUSE OF DRUG DEALING.

Summer 1999 had revealed how feeble the armed forces were. In April 2000, Kazakhstan, Kyrgyzstan, Tajikistan and Uzbekistan signed a treaty to combat terrorism, political and religious extremism and international organised crime. An attack on one was to be regarded as an attack on all. The most important strategic change was the attitude to Russia. Previously only Tajikistan had really needed Russia, now they all did. President Karimov, especially, had been very sarcastic in his anti-Russian comments. He told Moscow that he would teach Russians how to fight the Wahhabien. In December 1999, he talked about Chechnya being a 'base for international terrorism'. He immediately struck up a good relationship with President Putin and called Russia the 'backbone of the CIS'. Things had changed.

THE INSURGENTS RETURN

In August 1999, a jihad was proclaimed against President Karimov and his regime. Among the declared goals were an Islamic republic and the freeing of 50,000 Muslims from Karimov's jails (independent estimates put the number at about 7,000).

On 7 August 2000, the Uzbek government conceded that rebels under the command of Tahir Djoldashev and Djuma Namangani, leaders of the IMU, had entered the country from Tajikistan and were in Surkhan-Darya oblast, in the Fergana valley. There were also fighters from the Uzbek branch of the international Islamic organisation Hizb al Takhrir al-Islamy (the Party of Islamic Liberation which has a branch in Uzbekistan). One group occupied several Uzbek villages and another group took over a section of the road through the Kamchik pass and cut off part of the Fergana valley from Uzbekistan. A Tajik claimed that the rebels had come from Afghanistan. They had chosen Surkhan-Darya since it was very poor, overpopulated and had a Tajik majority.

On 11 August insurgents penetrated southern Kyrgyzstan and the Kyrgyz authorities feared they might make for the centre of the republic. An official claimed that there were many nationalities among the rebels: Uzbeks, Tajiks, Afghans, Pakistanis, Arabs, Chechens and even Ukrainians. This meant that the republic was confronted with international terrorism. A domino theory made its appearance. After Tajikistan, Kyrgyzstan and Uzbekistan would inevitably follow the southern areas of Kazakhstan. The alarmed

THE REPUBLIC WAS CONFRONTED WITH INTERNATIONAL TERRORISM.

Presidents saw themselves as the victims of an international chain of terrorism stretching from Chechnya to Central Asia and Afghanistan. After some clashes most of the insurgents returned to their Tajik base.

THE ISLAMIC MOVEMENT OF UZBEKISTAN

Since 1999 the IMU has become the most important Islamic and military threat to Uzbekistan and, indeed, the stability of the whole Central Asian region. Its name is misleading as its base is in Tajikistan and its origins go back to the civil wars in Tajikistan and Afghanistan. The poverty and over-population of the Fergana valley, in three states, favour its expansion. The adopted name of one of the leaders, Namangani, points to Namangan oblast as being the centre of the movement. There has always been opposition to President Karimov in the region. One of the reasons for this is that neither under the communists nor under Karimov have those from the region attained political influence in Uzbekistan. It has traditionally been the most religious part of the country. There were underground *madrasas* in the 1970s and 1980s and after 1991 Saudi and other missionaries and mullahs were frequent guests. They had become unwelcome guests by the mid-1990s, at least from the official point of view. Preachers from Saudi Arabia and Iran were deported from Uzbekistan and Turkmenistan in droves – 300 from Turkmenistan alone.

Bombs exploded in Tashkent in February 1999 and were officially blamed on Islamic terrorists. At least four Islamic organisations have been active since 1991: Hizb al-Takhrir (Party of Islamic Liberation); Adolat (Justice), Tovba (Repentance); and Islom Laskari (Army of Islam). Other fundamentalist Islamic organisations, such as Hizbollah and the Muslim Brotherhood were particularly active. Their relationship with the IMU is quite unclear. What is clear is that after President Karimov proscribed all religious parties and Islamic organisations, in 1992, their leaders moved to Tajikistan and Afghanistan. The major figures involved were Tahir Djoldashev (born 1968) and Djuma Namangani (born 1969). The former is regarded as the political leader and a mortal enemy of the present Uzbek regime. He was in the Middle East after 1991 and became associated with Adolat. This organisation protested about official neglect and engaged in self-help in the Fergana valley. An Adolat group had up to 200 members and there were 60 such groups in early 1992. They organised mass demonstrations at the end of 1991 in Namangan and President Karimov came personally to meet them. They demanded the proclamation of an Islamic republic. Karimov reacted to this challenge to his authority by banning Adolat and other Islamic organisations. This drove them underground. Hundreds of their members were jailed. Djoldashev and Namanagani moved to Tajikistan and joined the United Tajik Opposition. In February 1993, Djoldashev crossed into Afghanistan.

Namangani was the military leader and fought in Afghanistan as part of the Soviet armed forces in the late 1980s. His troops, apparently, were the main conduit for the smuggling of drugs and contraband from Afghanistan to Russia and Europe. Afghanistan produces enough opium to produce 350 tonnes of heroin annually, or about 75 per cent of world supply. Western Europe's annual consumption of heroin is about 120 tonnes and about 80 per cent of this emanates from Afghanistan. The couriers drive across the border in Chevrolet Blazers surrounded by their bodyguards equipped with state of the art night vision and communications gear.

80 PER CENT OF WESTERN EUROPE'S HEROIN EMANATES FROM AFGHANISTAN.

Each drug run is protected by 20 to 150 men. The Taliban (Mullah Omar) banned opium-producing poppy-growing in 2000 and told farmers to return to conventional crops. Fields were set on fire but the ban may have been a tactic to push up drug prices on western markets. The Taliban had huge stockpiles near the Pakistani border and were in danger of oversupplying the market. However the Northern Alliance, which controlled the northern 10 per cent of the country, continued to grow the poppies. Reducing supplies from Afghanistan had a dramatic effect on the price of a kilo of

A KILO OF RAW OPIUM ROSE FROM $30 IN 2000 TO $700 IN SEPTEMBER 2001

raw opium. It rose from $30 in 2000 to $700 in September 2001.

Border police have been more successful recently. In the first eight months of 2001 they seized 4.8 tonnes of opium and heroin. The drugs enter Tajikistan where the government is deeply involved in the trade. Some observers estimate that up to one third of the country's Gross Domestic Product comes from drugs. Then the route passes through Osh, Kyrgyzstan, and this would be one of the explanations as to why there was so much conflict there. The drug industry in Kyrgyzstan may have an annual turnover of $14 billion and the Afghan crop may be worth about $100 billion in street prices in the west. The availability of drugs has had a disastrous effect on neighbouring Muslim countries. Iran and Pakistan now have the highest rate of heroin addiction in the world. About 10 per cent of Iran's population may use drugs and the number of addicts is over 1 million. It is going to be very difficult to eliminate opium growing in Afghanistan as at least half the population depend on it for survival. The US does not view Afghan drugs as a problem – they only account for a minuscule part of the US narcotics industry.

Namangani returned to Afghanistan after the conflict in Kyrgyzstan and Uzbekistan. He was the commander of about 2,000 Uzbeks fighting with Taliban forces. He was wounded fighting opposition forces in Mazar-e Sharif, in November 2001. He was taken to Kabul for treatment but died of his wounds.

CONCLUSIONS

Under the communists the terms Islamism, fundamentalism and Wahhabism were used to vilify any manifestation of spirituality among Muslims. The alarm was always raised that believers were disguised agitators and even terrorists. There were some groups predisposed towards violence but it is not surprising that they found little support among the Muslims of Central Asia. This was to be expected after seventy years of atheistic propaganda. Raising the self-awareness and arousing the consciences of the region's Muslims would take time.

There have been three high points of activity since 1991:

- the emergence of the Islamic Renaissance Party, in the early 1990s, in Tajikistan. It became a political factor in the Tajik civil war. It also played a role in the clashes between local Islamic dissidents and the Uzbek authorities in the Fergana valley
- the advance of the Taliban in the mid-1990s
- the mini-wars in the Kyrgyz and Uzbek parts of the Fergana valley since 1999

Other factors which influenced the course of Islamic opposition were the war in Chechnya; the conflict in the Caucasus between the Wahhabien and the Tariquat (branch of Sufi order), the former more militant and the latter traditional to the region; and the turmoil in the Middle East, especially the Israeli–Palestinian issue. Overall there was a marked rise in the use of terror by Muslim groups. Afghanistan became a base for training Islamic militants, the al-Qaeda organisation. Those undergoing training were not only from Muslim states but also from Britain, the United States, Germany, France, Russia, China and others.

AFGHANISTAN BECAME A BASE FOR TRAINING ISLAMIC MILITANTS, THE AL-QAEDA ORGANISATION.

Various conclusions can be reached about Islam in Central Asia during the 1990s:

- The role of Islam in political life is increasing. This is especially marked in Uzbekistan and Turkmenistan because religious protest is the only form of dissent left after the criminalisation of secular dissent. There are political parties but they are merely cosmetic to please the outside world which would like to see a multi-party system developing everywhere. In 1991, some observers doubted whether Central Asia was a part of the *ummah*, the world community of Islam. There is now no doubt. Attitudes towards the Taliban, until 1999, were quite moderate. Even in Uzbekistan the objectives of the Taliban were discussed in measured tones. The Tashkent bombs of February 1999 (viewed as attempts to murder President Karimov) and the Islamic invasion of the Batken region in August 1999 changed all that. Now the Taliban became terrorists.
- Attention has been concentrated on Tajikistan, Uzbekistan and Kyrgyzstan as the epicentre of the problem. Part of the Tajik–Afghan border was open to the Taliban and this caused grave concern about the penetration of the Taliban or Taliban-supported mujahidin into Tajikistan and other states. This fear was given stimulus by the fact that Djuma Namangani was also a Taliban commander. By 2000, 'religious extremism' dominated discussions about national security in Uzbekistan. It began to affect all other states with the exception of Turkmenistan. Before 1999, it was low in the list of national security problems but then it became

one of the most serious. The difficulty of creating a Kazakhstani identity from so many ethnic groups was a factor of instability in the republic. However traditionally Islam has always been moderate there. Nevertheless the extreme poverty of the heavily populated southern Kazakhstan provided a breeding ground for radical Islamic solutions. President Nazarbaev is now wont to pillory religious extremism and Wahhibism. He views these as the greatest threat to the stability of the whole Central Asian region. In Kyrgyzstan, the battle of Batken has transformed views about the 'Islamic danger'. Turkmenistan is the exception as Turkmenbashi has sought to remain neutral in the conflict in Afghanistan and to maintain good relations with the Taliban. Bashi has arranged that prayers to Allah are followed by prayers for his wellbeing. Since the country is a one-man show, his removal would provoke instability from which Islamic groups would benefit.

• Leaders of the Central Asian states have attempted to develop their own brand of Islam. However the nationalisation of Islam has not taken place. Indeed religious development in each state has been quite different. The centre of Islamic activity is the Fergana valley where 40 per cent of the population of the region live. Uzbekistan has attempted to integrate and mould Islam. The official view is that Islam in Uzbekistan is indigenous and is a special variant of Islam. It is quite independent of other forms, such as those in

THE NATIONALISATION OF ISLAM HAS NOT TAKEN PLACE . . . RELIGIOUS DEVELOPMENT IN EACH STATE HAS BEEN QUITE DIFFERENT.

Turkey and Iran. Islam is inextricably linked to the nation and acts as a mobiliser in developing the nation and state. It promotes economic development and the rule of law. In Uzbekistan, it is a bridging mechanism between the Third World and the Second World (China, India, South Korea). This vision is of a secular Islam. Unsurprisingly, it is vigorously opposed by Islamic dissidents.

FOUR

THE GREAT GAME:
THE POWERS VIE
FOR PRIMACY

AFGHANISTAN: THE COCKPIT

Afghanistan is the cockpit of Asia. Modernisation has fuelled all the conflicts within the country in the twentieth century. It is a classic example of a state attempting to move in the direction of the most successful world states, and failing to make the transition. Before 1917, the only model was a western, capitalist one. Britain was the most successful country and attracted most interest. Afghanistan had to bow the knee to British imperialist power. This caused enormous resentment among its proud inhabitants. The question was how to become stronger in order to throw off the British yoke. The problem was that the country's Islamic identity collided with attempts to introduce secular reforms. Reform or modernisation begins with education.

Secular training needs to begin as early as possible in a child's life. However, this was perceived as a dangerous heresy by Muslim clerics. The more secular the population

THE COUNTRY'S ISLAMIC IDENTITY COLLIDED WITH ATTEMPTS TO INTRODUCE SECULAR REFORMS.

became, the less influence they would enjoy. There were English, French and German lycées in Kabul but they were only attended by a small section of Afghan society. They were secular with foreign teachers and they taught in their own language. Afghans have great linguistic ability and quickly master foreign languages. The extent to which they adopt the values expressed in the foreign language is quite a different matter.

Much advice was dispensed and aid extended by the Americans in order to promote economic development. A key sector was agriculture since the vast majority of Afghans are subsistence farmers. Canals were built and land irrigated but the net result was disappointing. It proved particularly difficult to convince farmers to espouse new methods and produce increasing surpluses for the market. Why take the risk? Why market the surplus when they needed to consume more themselves? Given the extremes of temperatures in the country, working in a factory is not very attractive. American economic endeavour produced modest returns. The population was just not receptive to new, foreign ideas.

THE POPULATION WAS JUST NOT RECEPTIVE TO NEW, FOREIGN IDEAS.

The other power which believed it had an unbeatable model was the Soviet Union. All it had to do was to adapt practices honed in Central Asia to Afghanistan. Collective farms and state-driven industrial development looked good on paper. Soviet engineers and specialists were there to help and a new generation of specialists was being trained in the USSR. As it turned out, optimism was misplaced. Virulent opposition from the clerics and a miserably low level of education slowed the transition. Another major weakness was the arrogance of the young communists who believed they could modernise their country very rapidly. They did not believe they had to win the support of the population in order to push through their very radical reforms. These reforms had as their goal a secular society in the country. The other factor was that the communists could not agree among themselves – the age-old weakness of the Afghans.

The fiercely independent nature of the people, the binding family and tribal loyalties, and the isolation of the country has contributed to the rejection of both the capitalist and communist models of development.

> THE FIERCELY INDEPENDENT NATURE OF THE PEOPLE, HAS CONTRIBUTED TO THE REJECTION OF BOTH THE CAPITALIST AND COMMUNIST MODELS OF DEVELOPMENT.

Afghanistan is now in a position to start again on the long road to a better standard of living for all its citizens. There is now only one credible model – the capitalist. Marxist economics has failed and the country has to adopt measures which have proved successful elsewhere. Again the most important barrier to modernisation, which also means secularisation, will be constructed by the Muslim clergy. The challenge for the new government and its advisers will be to conceive of policies which are acceptable to the clergy as well as to lay people. As before, Afghans will not tolerate foreign advisers dictating to them how they should work and live. It is a formidable challenge. The Afghan authorities cannot afford to

AFGHANS WILL NOT TOLERATE FOREIGN
ADVISERS DICTATING TO THEM HOW
THEY SHOULD WORK AND LIVE.

fail, as failure would
mean the return of
the Taliban and 'pure'
Islam. The oppor-
tunity to develop a secular state has never been greater. It has
to be seized and foreign powers need to provide resources and
advice – skilfully fashioned for Afghan ears. Foreign states
need to agree among themselves what they will collectively
do. There is little room for them to compete with one other
for influence.

CENTRAL ASIA

Central Asia was thrust onto the world stage in December
1979 when Soviet troops invaded Afghanistan. Tajikistan,
Turkmenistan and Uzbekistan provided bases for the decade-
long conflict. Previously only specialists were acquainted
with the region. When Soviet power collapsed in 1991 the
powers vied for precedence in the region. It was strategically
important in that it lay between China and Russia. Russia,
the traditional source of influence, did not favour any other
power penetrating its backyard. From the Muslim point of
view, Turkey, Saudi Arabia, Pakistan and Iran competed for
precedence. The Iranian revolution of 1979, which had sig-
nalled the rejection of a western model of development,
might inspire a similar anti-western model in Central Asia.
The United States favoured strong states emerging in Central
Asia which would prove a barrier to Russian expansion in the
area. However, had no hydrocarbons been discovered in
Central Asia it would have remained a relative backwater
after 1991. The abundance of oil and gas meant that it

acquired great strategic import-ance. The west needs these

HAD NO HYDROCARBONS BEEN DISCOVERED IN CENTRAL ASIA IT WOULD HAVE REMAINED A RELATIVE BACKWATER AFTER 1991.

sources of energy as its voracious appetite grows. They could supplement or even become alternative sources to those of the volatile Middle East. China and the west need the hydro-carbons and have to ensure the region's stability. An Islamic revolution might cut them off from the outside world. The new Muslim masters might deny them to the outside world in the ongoing struggle by Islamic radicals to weaken the non-Muslim world.

The armed forces of the Central Asian states are weak and quite incapable of defending the national territory. Kazakhstan's frontiers stretch for over 15,000 km and, not surpris-ingly, its military is quite incapable of

THE ARMED FORCES OF CENTRAL ASIA ARE WEAK AND QUITE INCAPABLE OF DEFENDING THE NATIONAL TERRITORY.

defending them. Kyrgyzstan's military performance against Islamic warriors in 1999 and 2000 was woeful. Tajikistan could not have survived the conflict against the United Tajik Opposition without the support of Russia. After 1997, the policy of reconciliation led to the integration of UTO fight-ers in the Tajik national forces. At present these forces are incapable of defending the state. Turkmenistan has remained outside all collective agreements and favours bilateral treaties. It maintained good relations with the Taliban while it was in power in Afghanistan. Uzbekistan has the largest army but found it difficult to deal with insurgents in 1999 and 2000.

Central Asia has not developed a national security identity or been integrated into a major international security organisation. Bilateral and multilateral treaties have been the norm. President Karimov of Uzbekistan has pointed to this weakness as a major geopolitical factor influencing present day thinking. A treaty of collective security was signed by all states, except Turkmenistan, in May 1992, in Tashkent. This was part of the CIS security architecture. Uzbekistan left in 1999 stating that it was of little consequence. One of the reasons for its lack of success was the fear of Russian military dominance. A Central Asian Economic Union, modelled on the European Union, came into existence in 1994 but remained in embryo. Its members, Kazakhstan, Kyrgyzstan and Uzbekistan had difficulty cooperating. The penetration of Kyrgyzstan and Uzbekistan by Islamic insurgents, from their bases in Tajikistan, did not lead to closer security relations. Instead both states began fortifying their frontiers as mutual suspicion grew. This ran counter to efforts to establish an economic common market.

A CENTRAL ASIAN ECONOMIC UNION, CAME INTO EXISTENCE IN 1994. ITS MEMBERS HAD DIFFICULTY COOPERATING.

The most successful inter-regional collaboration has been within the Shanghai Five group (China, Russia, Kazakhstan, Kyrgyzstan and Tajikistan). After Uzbekistan joined it has become the Shanghai Forum. It began, in April 1996, as a group of states trying to resolve outstanding border disputes and gradually developed into an organisation with a common interest in combating Islamic terrorism and religious extremism. China is faced with the challenge of separatists in the

Xinjiang Uigur autonomous region. They have received training in al-Qaeda camps in Afghanistan and fought with the Taliban against the Northern Alliance in late 2001. However, border disputes continue to plague member states. In 1999, Uzbekistan began demarcating sections of its border with Kazakhstan. This led to an official protest by Kazakhstan and Uzbek forces have fired on Kazakhs in the border area. Turkmenistan's borders with Uzbekistan and Kazakhstan are not clear and this takes on added significance because of the wealth which may lie under the burning sands.

The struggle against international terrorism has provided the impetus, for the first time, to fashion a common response in Central Asia and the CIS. Central Asian and other CIS states have participated in joint military manoeuvres in Tajikistan, Kyrgyzstan and Uzbekistan. However, there are limits to this new-found enthusiasm to integrate. Uzbekistan has withdrawn its appeals for Russian military aid even though it accepted some from China. The shadow in the background was always the Taliban which dominated Afghanistan in 1996–2001.

CHINA

China's interest in Central Asia is growing. The region will play an increasing role in international affairs because of its mineral and energy wealth. China is energy-poor and needs to import more and more as its economy grows. The country has problems with Islamic groups whose goals are religious and

CHINA IS ENERGY-POOR AND NEEDS TO IMPORT MORE AND MORE AS ITS ECONOMY GROWS.

separatist. A stable and prosperous Central Asia is in Beijing's interests. However, there are various scenarios which would be inimical to China's interests. These include Central Asia coming closer to the Middle East with Islam playing a more important role in policy. Russian domination might exclude China. American hegemony might do the same. In this respect, China is concerned about the eastward expansion of NATO and the fact that all Central Asian states (except Tajikistan) are members of the Partnership for Peace (PfP) programme.

Mikhail Gorbachev improved relations with China and swiftly moved to find a solution to the border question. The eastern border was more or less agreed but the western border was left untouched. China has a 3,000 km border with Kazakhstan, Kyrgyzstan and Tajikistan. In April 1994, Li Peng, the Chinese Prime Minister, and President Nazarbaev of Kazakhstan signed an agreement covering most of the 1,700 km border. Other accords were signed in 1997 and 1998 which almost resolved all the outstanding disagreements. However, Kazakhstan has been concerned to see that in Chinese schoolbooks the western boundary of the country includes parts of Kazakhstan. The Kyrgyz–Chinese border was more or less agreed in 1996 and, in 1999, China, Kazakhstan and Kyrgyzstan signed an additional agreement which reinforced previous treaties. However the Chinese–Tajik border issue has not been resolved as there is a complex dis-

KAZAKHSTAN HAS BEEN CONCERNED TO SEE THAT IN CHINESE SCHOOLBOOKS THE WESTERN BOUNDARY OF THE COUNTRY INCLUDES PARTS OF KAZAKHSTAN.

pute over the ownership of over 20,000 square km in the Pamirs. Kazakhstan was a nuclear power under the communists. It was reluctant to give up its weapons, given its weak military position. However, after receiving security guarantees from China, Russia and the United States, Kazakhstan passed all its remaining nuclear weapons to Russia. The Shanghai Five agreement, signed in April 1996, had, as one its objectives, confidence-building measures, especially in the security sphere. In 1997, an agreement was signed on reducing military forces in border areas.

In 1993, China became a net importer of oil and this spurred its interest in Central Asia. In June 1997, the China National Petroleum Company (CNPC) acquired the Uzen oilfield in Kazakhstan. This agreement has since lapsed. The CNPC is now working on exploiting three oilfields in Aktyubinsk oblast. The major problem was how to ship Kazakh oil to China. At present it goes by rail. In 1997, a potentially huge investment decision was taken by CNPC when it signed an agreement to build a 3,000 km pipeline from western Kazakhstan to western China. The CNPC has also agreed to build a pipeline from the Uzen region of Kazakhstan to the Turkmenistan border.

Trade expanded in the second half of the 1990s. China is now the second largest trading partner of Kazakhstan and Kyrgyzstan. In 1992, the railway between Urumchi, Xinjiang and Almaty, Kazakhstan began operation. Many other border crossings have been opened since then. A major complaint of the Chinese is that Central Asian states engage in barter because of lack of hard currency.

Islamism and separatism are problems for China in the Xinjiang Uighur autonomous region which borders on Central Asia. Of the 16.6 million population, 7 million are Uighurs, who are Turkic and Muslim. The visitor is amazed to see beautiful blonde women who would pass for Scandinavians. They turn out to be Uighur. There are also about 1 million Kazakhs in Xinjiang as well as Kyrgyz and Tajiks. Political Islam became a problem in the 1970s and mid-1980s as many Muslims rediscovered their faith. These included communist party officials and university teachers and students. By the mid-1980s, Xinjiang had the largest number of mosques to believers in the world – about one to every 150 worshippers. Radical Islam appeared in the second half of the 1980s. Schools (*madrasas*) were opened to educate a new Islamic élite and the population was encouraged to ignore the Chinese authorities and follow the precepts of the Sharia. The situation changed for the worse in the 1990s when radicals began to engage in violence. Various groups favour independence for Xinjiang. This has been stimulated by the independence of the Central Asian states but also by the Taliban's success in Afghanistan. Separatists are most active in Kazakhstan and have organisations in Turkey and Germany. Uighur fighters have been trained in al-Qaeda camps in Afghanistan. The Shanghai Forum now seeks to coordinate efforts to combat terrorism and religious extremism.

> THE VISITOR IS AMAZED TO SEE BEAUTIFUL BLONDE WOMEN WHO WOULD PASS FOR SCANDINAVIANS. THEY TURN OUT TO BE UIGHUR.

RUSSIA

Russia's domestic problems have taken precedence over its relations with Central Asia. President Boris Yeltsin was faced with two main options after he had conspired with Ukraine and Belarus to bring the Soviet Union to an end in 1991. Russia could attempt to replace the Soviet Union and become the main engine of political and economic change in the Commonwealth of Independent States (CIS). The other choice was to walk away from the other CIS states and go it alone. In choosing Egor Gaidar and his policy of shock therapy – moving to a market economy in the shortest possible time – he was choosing to abandon the CIS. Gaidar had little time for Central Asia and regarded it as a drag on Russia's development. However, the region stayed within the Russian ruble zone until 1994. This meant that Russia was effectively subsidising Central Asia as the Russian Central Bank met all the ruble bills the new states ran up.

There were originally CIS armed forces but the member states were wary of Russian ambitions and this quickly faded away. National armed forces took over. Various agreements were signed regarding collective security but meant little in reality, given the straightened economic circumstances of all states. Things appeared to change in 1993 when Russia renewed the pursuit of its own national interests. There was talk of Russia becoming a great power again. It remained just talk. President Yeltsin signed a decree, in September 1995, establishing a CIS political, economic and defence union. It never came to anything because Russia could not afford it financially. The Central Asian states had been looking forward to receiving desperately needed subsidies. Another reason why the proposed union failed to materialise was that Central Asian states were unwilling to be integrated in multilateral structures. They wanted all the economic benefits but were not willing to give up any sovereignty. After having escaped from the imperialist Russian bear, it is understandable that they were loath to be hugged too closely by the new democratic bear. Evgeny Primakov, Russia's deft foreign minister and later Prime Minister, was quite pragmatic. Relations were to be based on economic interest. Russia helped the various countries set up their armed forces and Russian troops stayed in several states to ensure stability. The civil war in Tajikistan, which began in 1992, sucked Russia in. Without Russian military aid and troops Tajikistan could not have withstood the rebels. The 201st motorised division (now down to 11,000 men) was deployed to guard the frontier with Afghanistan and 20,000 other Russian troops are stationed elsewhere in the country.

Russia had two security objectives: dominate the region and prevent any foreign power gaining influence. Moscow regarded Pakistan, Iran, Turkey, Saudi Arabia, the United States and NATO as actors who wished to expand their presence in the area at the expense of Russia. Central Asian states did not view these states as a threat but as an opportunity to secure investment. As a result they would become less dependent on Russia. Anyway Russia did not have the resources to invest in the area so foreign investment would have to come from outside Russia.

From a military point of view, Central Asian leaders were always sceptical about Russian military plans for integration. Instead they have fashioned relationships with western states within the NATO Partnership for Peace programme. Joint military exercises, involving NATO soldiers, now take place on Central Asian territory and Central Asian officers also receive training in the United States. The new Russian national security concept of February 2000 sets out to combat rising US and western influence in the Caucasus and Central Asia. Persistent western criticism of Russia's conduct of the first Chechen war of 1994–96 and the second, which began in 1999, irked the Russian military.

Russia quickly linked the conflict in Chechnya to that in Afghanistan and Central Asia, in 1999. Moscow's concern is that political and radical Islam should not penetrate the Volga region where there are two Muslim republics, Tatarstan and Bashkortostan. In the former, in 2001, one could hear calls for an Islamic republic.

PIPELINES

The Russians have a very important card they can play in the poker game of oil and gas supplies. Until recently they had a monopoly over the export of oil and gas: hydrocarbons had to flow through Russia and Russia owns the pipelines. A pipeline, built by the Caspian Pipeline Consortium, costing $2.6 billion, to carry oil from the Kazakh oilfields in Tengiz to Novorossiisk, on the Black Sea, was begun in 1999 and the first oil passed through in late October 2001. Its initial capacity is 28.2 million tonnes a year (560,000 barrels per day) but its final capacity will be 67 million tonnes. This is the first step in Kazakhstan's ambitious plan to deliver 3 million barrels a day in 15 years and become one of the top three oil-exporting countries in the world.

KAZAKHSTAN'S AMBITIOUS PLAN IS TO BECOME ONE OF THE TOP THREE OIL-EXPORTING COUNTRIES IN THE WORLD.

Another Russian oil pipeline ran from Baku, Azerbaijan, to Novorossiisk. However, as it ran through Chechnya it soon failed. The Russians have replaced the Chechnya link with a pipeline through Dagestan and the first oil reached Novorossiisk in November 2001. As oil and gas producers did not wish to be beholden only to Russia many new pipeline projects surfaced. There were proposals to carry hydrocarbons to the east (China), to the south (through Afghanistan and Iran) and to the west (Ceyhan, on the Turkish Mediterranean coast). They are still at the planning stage because of the huge financial costs, the political uncertainty and the volume to be exported. Then there is the price of oil. On paper many of these projects are making progress. In November 1999, the Presidents of Turkmenistan, Azerbaijan, Georgia and Turkey signed a memorandum of understanding to construct the pipeline to Ceyhan. However, as any businessman knows, a memorandum of understanding is only a piece of paper which does not bind anyone to do anything.

Another memorandum of understanding was signed at the same meeting, in February 1999, to build a Transcaspian gas

AS ANY BUSINESSMAN KNOWS, A MEMORANDUM OF UNDERSTANDING IS ONLY A PIECE OF PAPER WHICH DOES NOT BIND ANYONE TO DO ANYTHING.

pipeline to take gas from Turkmenistan to Turkey. Gazprom, the Russian gas monopoly, wants to build a gas pipeline across the Black Sea to carry Russian gas to Turkey. Clearly there is not enough demand in Turkey for both projects.

PEACEKEEPING

Some Kyrgyz and Uzbek forces helped in Tajikistan. Russia was keen to develop an integrated peacekeeping force (the Russian word for peacekeeping actually means peace making) for the region. This received a cool reception and, in 1996, Kazakhstan, Kyrgyzstan and Uzbekistan set up their own national peacekeeping forces. They began cooperating with one another and also with the PfP programme. There are now no Russian military forces in Uzbekistan. In February 1999, Uzbekistan declared that it would not renew its membership of the CIS collective security treaty. Instead it joined Georgia, Ukraine, Uzbekistan, Azerbaijan, Moldova, the GUUAM group. It began to look as if Uzbekistan were moving out of the Russian military orbit. This was not entirely so. The rise of political and radical Islam led to Russia, Tajikistan and Uzbekistan agreeing to cooperate, in May 1998. Another agreement was signed later in the year and this time there was a clause on military assistance in the event of aggression. In July 1999, a further agreement widened the scope to include combating drug and arms dealers. The attack on Osh, Kyrgyzstan, in August 1999, alarmed everyone and when President Putin visited Uzbekistan, in December 1999 and May 2000, more agreements were signed. Putin stated dramatically that joint efforts were under way to prevent the spread of 'terrorism and extremism'. The CIS summit, in June 2000, adopted the relevant measures and also agreed to establish an anti-terrorist centre.

THE CIS SUMMIT, IN JUNE 2000, AGREED TO ESTABLISH AN ANTI-TERRORIST CENTRE.

In Turkmenistan, Russian troops were responsible for patrolling the border with Afghanistan and Iran, from 1993 onwards. In May 1999, Turkmenistan unilaterally announced that it was terminating the border agreement since the Russians had now completed their work. Russian border guards left Turkmenistan in December 1999. Turkmenistan is officially a neutral state but regards cooperation with the PfP programme as consistent with its neutrality. In May 1999, it signed an agreement continuing cooperation with the PfP programme. There are still Russian troops along the Kazakhstan–China border but they are gradually giving way to Kazakh border guards. In Tajikistan, the Kazakh, Kyrgyz and Uzbek peacekeeping forces, part of the CIS peacekeeping force, left in 1998. In June 2000, the CIS mandate lapsed. Since Tajikistan wanted Russian troops to stay, an agreement was signed, in April 1999, which will see the 201st motorised division forming part of a Russian military base. Putin has made clear that Russian troops will stay in the country as long as is necessary. The Russians now have installations to track aircraft and satellites there.

IRAN

The 1979 revolution in Iran was a watershed in the Middle East. Previously modernisation, understood as the American model, was regarded as the way forward for Islamic states. The intense opposition to the Shah's policy of overt Americanisation offended deeply the country's Shiite clerics. They rightly perceived that continuing modernisation would gradually sideline them. The Ayatollah Khomeini inspired a counter-revolution that reversed the trend and Iran became a cleric-dominated state. The new rulers regarded the change as a victory for Islam over the infidel. There were two great enemies: the great Satan was the United States and the little Satan was Israel. To the north was the red Satan, the Soviet communists who held sway in Central Asia and the Caucasus, traditionally Muslim regions (except Georgia and Armenia). Buoyed up with religious fervour, it appeared Iran could undermine the secular Muslim regimes in the Middle East. Saddam Hussein, the Iraqi dictator, was quick to sense the danger and war broke out between the two countries in 1980. There were heavy causalities on both sides before it ended as a draw in 1988. The US helped the Iraqis. The war taught Tehran several lessons. The main one was that involvement in military conflict beyond its borders could seriously destabilise the country and could lead to the defeat of the ruling clerics. Henceforth Iran became very cautious and restricted itself to supporting terrorist groups outside the country. Most attention was paid to economic and social

> THERE WERE TWO GREAT ENEMIES: THE GREAT SATAN WAS THE UNITED STATES AND THE LITTLE SATAN WAS ISRAEL.

development under Ayatollah Khomeini (died 1989) and during the presidency of Ali Akhbar Rafsanjani (1989–97). President Mohammad Khatami, elected in 1997, has been pursuing a more liberal policy at home. He has also been attempting to improve relations with Washington and other western states.

Iran had some links with Central Asia before the collapse of communism in 1991 but was, on the whole, woefully ill-informed about the region. Immediately after 1991 Iran entered into vigorous competition with Turkey for influence. Iran feared that if Turkey became very influential this would provide a back door for American influence. The continuing conflict between Azerbaijan and Armenia over Nagorno-Karabakh threatened to spill over into Iran. There is a large Azeri minority in northern Iran. The civil war in Tajikistan, the troubled situation in Afghanistan and the ever-present threat of Iraq (reinforced by Iraq's invasion of Kuwait in 1991) changed Iran's perception of foreign policy. It concluded that its best interests would be served by dropping its ideological approach and promoting stability and normal state-to-state relations with countries in the Middle East and Central Asia. A nightmarish scenario could become reality if the south

IRAN CONCLUDED THAT ITS BEST INTERESTS WOULD BE SERVED BY PROMOTING STABILITY AND NORMAL STATE-TO-STATE RELATIONS.

Caucasus, Central Asia and Afghanistan all descended into bloody anarchy. Iraq remains the most serious threat and it provides bases for the Mojaheddin-e Khalq organisation which carries out terrorist attacks in Iran. It irks Tehran that the US views Iraq and Iran as the two rogue states of the Middle East, ignoring the fact that Iraq poses a security threat to Iran.

Iran and Turkey had mistakenly thought that Central Asia was a vacuum but soon discovered that Moscow regarded the region as its own backyard. Turkey suggested it could serve as a source of investment and a conduit to the west. It transpired that neither Iran nor Turkey had the resources to promote economic development in the region. The Central Asian states also made it clear that they did not want a conduit to the west, they wanted to deal directly with western states.

Another factor for Tehran and Ankara was that pursuing their ambition for greater influence in Central

> **THE CENTRAL ASIAN STATES DID NOT WANT A CONDUIT, THEY WANTED TO DEAL DIRECTLY WITH WESTERN STATES.**

Asia would conflict with their desired goals of improving relations with the new rulers in Moscow. Eventually both decided that relations with Russia took precedence over those of Central Asia.

Russia was one of Iran's main sources of war material and of fulfilling its ambition to become a nuclear power. A ten-year weapons agreement was signed in 1989 and a nuclear agreement in 1995. This has exercised American minds but, even during the heady days of the Boris Yeltsin and Bill Clinton show, Moscow held to its policy of supplying Tehran with arms and nuclear parts. Iran has therefore been circumspect in its relations with Russia. For instance, in the late 1980s, when it was considering setting up consulates in Central

Asia, it enquired first in Moscow if this were acceptable. It has taken a pragmatic approach to Central Asia ever since and has never sought advantage which would antagonise Russia.

There were regular visits by Iranian foreign ministers and others and this facilitated a closer understanding. One of the criticisms of Turkey's involvement was that foreign ministers changed all the time and every new one had to start from scratch in building up relationships. Until 1993, Iran and state-sponsored Islamic foundations attempted to promote a resurgence of Islam. Many clerics preached and taught in the region. The fact that the Iranian clerics were Shiites whereas most Muslims in Central Asia are Sunnis did not seem to be very important. Iran helped to set up *madrasas* and mosques. Students were encouraged to study in Iran.

President Rafsanjani concentrated on promoting economic links with Central Asia. It was not easy as both had under-developed economies which concentrated on the export of commodities such as oil. However, progress was

PRESIDENT RAFSANJANI CONCENTRATED ON PROMOTING ECONOMIC LINKS WITH CENTRAL ASIA.

made. New crossings on the border with Afghanistan were opened, new shipping routes were added between Iran's Caspian Sea ports and Turkmenistan and Kazakhstan and new air routes linked Iran and Central Asia. A direct connection between the Iranian and Central Asian railway networks was opened in May 1996. A 300 km rail link between northern Iran and Turkmenistan achieved this. A 200 km pipeline permitted the direct export of Turkmen gas to Iran. The project was financed by Iran and was envisaged as the first stage in the supply of Turkmen gas to Turkey and Europe. This has not materialised as northern Iran needs all the gas. President Niyazov has maintained friendly relations with Iran. There are about 1.5 million Turkmen living in Iran but no irredentist movement has appeared and Niyazov has never attempted to play the ethnic card. An oil pipeline on Iran's Caspian Sea coast to Tehran will permit a great expansion of oil swaps between Kazakhstan and Iran. The latter imports Kazakhstani oil for its northern refineries and exports an equivalent amount of Iranian oil, the income going to the Kazakhs. Iran does have modest stakes in some Azerbaijani oil companies but has not yet broken through to become a major oil player in the Caspian Sea area. Disputes continue between Iran and Azerbaijan and Turkmenistan about the development of Caspian Sea resources.

The Economic Cooperation Organisation (ECO) is an important vehicle for Iran's economic interests. In 1992, the Central Asian states and Afghanistan joined the three original members, Iran, Turkey and Pakistan to create a new regional body to promote trade and investment. The secretariat is in Tehran. There are agreements to promote transport and communications links within the group and to fight drug trafficking and organised crime. If a peaceful settlement can be achieved in Afghanistan and Iran's relations with the US improve, many pipeline projects, carrying Central Asian oil and gas to the Indian Ocean and the Persian Gulf, are possible. The future looks promising.

TURKEY

To the Turks, Central Asia excludes Tajikistan but includes Turkmen and Uzbek-populated territory in northern Afghanistan and Xinjiang, where Turkic-speaking Uigurs live. Ankara has almost ignored Farsi-speaking Tajikistan even though there is a substantial minority of Uzbeks in the country. Turkey is indirectly affected by what happens in Central Asia as the Caucasus is of more immediate relevance. However Turkey has concluded military agreements with Central Asian states and, as a NATO member, plays an important role in the possible expansion of NATO into the region. All Turkic countries are members of NATO's Partnership for Peace programme. Russia's renewed war with Chechnya is a cause of concern for Turkey as it radicalises Islam and sows the seed of instability next door.

> TURKEY, AS A NATO MEMBER, PLAYS AN IMPORTANT ROLE IN THE POSSIBLE EXPANSION OF NATO INTO CENTRAL ASIA.

Ankara was quick off the mark in 1992 to promote the Turkish model of development. The Prime Minister got carried away and spoke of a huge Turkic world stretching from the Adriatic to the Great Wall of China. There was talk of setting up an association of independent Turkic states. The United States had no objection because an expansion of Turkish influence would hold back a rise in Iranian influence. The euphoria lasted until October 1992 when the first Turkic conference produced meagre results. Turkey was insensitive to the needs of the new states. They had no intention of swopping one big brother for another, Russia for Turkey. At the end of the day Turkey did not have the financial clout to make much of an impact. Turkish companies did much more business in Russia than in Central Asia. By the end of 1997 construction companies had fulfilled contracts worth $5.75 billion in Central Asia compared to $12.3 billion in Russia. The latter was also a much more important trade partner. Turkey, of course, actively supports the construction of a Caspian Pipeline Consortium pipeline from Baku, Azerbaijan, to Tbilisi, Georgia, and to Ceyhan, on the Mediterranean coast. It will cost about $2.5 billion to build. However, to break even, the pipeline needs a throughput of at least 45 million tonnes of oil a year. In order for this amount of oil to pass through, a pipeline under the Caspian carrying Kazakhstani oil would be necessary. However, Tengiz oil has begun flowing along a pipeline to Novorossiisk, on the Russian Black Sea coast. There are plans to build another one.

Central Asian states and Turkey have been exchanging military delegations since 1993. In 1998, the deputy chief of the Turkish general staff, stated that about 2,300 cadets and officers from Central Asia and Transcaucasia had graduated from Turkey's war colleges, and another 1,700 were still undergoing training. In that year, Turkmenistan had over 1,000 military personnel undergoing instruction in Turkey. Kazakhstan and Turkey signed an agreement on military industrial cooperation, in 1996. It is now actively involved in

IN 1998, TURKMENISTAN HAD OVER 1,000 MILITARY PERSONNEL UNDERGOING INSTRUCTION IN TURKEY.

arms production projects with Central Asian states but direct arms exports remain modest.

There is cooperation in combating religious extremism and organised crime. Ankara was exercised by the fact that the Kurdish guerrilla group, the Kurdish Workers' Party (PKK), was active in Kyrgyzstan. In April 1998, the Kyrgyz government assured Turkey that its activities would cease. Since 1997, Turkey has been a member of the six (Central Asia and Turkey) plus two group (Russia and the United States) attempting to broker a peaceful settlement to the crisis in Afghanistan. Turkey has been closely linked to the Uzbek warlord General Abdul Rashid Dostum who was in exile there in the late 1990s. Turkish officers visited Mazar-e Sharif. In August and September 1998, Dostum and the ousted Afghan President Burhanuddin Rabbani visited Ankara and asked Turkey to urge Pakistan to stop backing the Taliban. Nothing came of this initiative.

President Karimov of Uzbekistan complained to Turkey about the presence of the exiled Uzbek opposition leader, Mohammed Salih. He had to leave Turkey in early 1999. Relations have not been on an even keel of late. Tashkent has closed 12 Turkish schools and recalled 234 Uzbek students studying in Turkey. This was in response to Turkish slowness in extraditing two Uzbeks suspected of involvement in the bomb attacks in Tashkent, in February 1999. Uzbek authorities were annoyed by the activities of some Turkish businessmen who had been promoting Islamic radicalism in Uzbekistan. There are over

RELATIONS HAVE NOT BEEN ON AN EVEN KEEL OF LATE.

15,000 Uigurs in Turkey who sympathise with the aspirations of their ethnic kin in Xinjiang. China has warned Turkey not to interfere in its domestic affairs.

Turkey is a useful military ally of the United States in Central Asia. However should Islamic parties gain ascendancy in Turkey the situation would change completely. Turkey needs economic growth to weaken the attractiveness of Islamic solutions to the present economic and social problems.

UNITED STATES

Oil is what makes American pulses race. It was not always so. For instance in Kazakhstan, after independence, the United States was only concerned with getting nuclear weapons and equipment out of it.

> OIL IS WHAT MAKES AMERICAN PULSES RACE. IT WAS NOT ALWAYS SO.

By 1994, Washington had woken up to the fact that the region had enormous hydrocarbon potential. Of course, America pushed its own model of development, the expansion of democracy, a liberal market economy, the rule of law and so on. The problem was that these axioms held little appeal for the ex-communist leaders of Central Asia. In 1994–95 Washington's policy was based on hard-headed realism. The first objective was to prevent Russia monopolising Central Asian energy development, especially the Caspian Sea basin. This went hand in hand with stopping Russia gaining military ascendancy there. Another goal was to reduce Iran's influence to a minimum. Hence America strongly favoured pipelines to Turkey which would break the

existing Russian export monopoly. The United States inti-
mated that it would come to the aid of Central Asian states
if Russia tried oil blackmail. America aimed to make the
Caucasus and Central Asia its own zone of influence and
ensure international competition. The major drawback of
this policy is that it involves Washington in every dispute,
from Nagorno-Karabakh to Islamic insurgency in Kyrgyzstan.

The pursuit of democracy, beneficial though it may be, has
quietly been pushed down the agenda in favour of economic
and military interests. Pro-democracy programmes have
had little impact as regional leaders see them as promoting opposition. The major reason for this is that, para-
doxically, their hydrocarbon wealth impedes democracy

THE PURSUIT OF DEMOCRACY, HAS
QUIETLY BEEN PUSHED DOWN THE
AGENDA IN FAVOUR OF ECONOMIC
AND MILITARY INTERESTS.

and the growth of a liberal market economy. Since the in-situ
leaderships envisage greater and greater wealth from hydrocarbons and minerals, they resist any change which weakens
their monopoly hold on resources. National companies dominate the economy. Why should they permit the expansion
of foreign investment if this is going to loosen their control of
their economies? Hence one can argue that the authoritarian
leaders are acting rationally. They have got their hands on
their states' wealth and intend holding on. Hydrocarbon and
mineral extraction do not require a huge infrastructure (like
advanced technological industries) and, anyway, foreign
expertise can be brought in.

PAKISTAN

Pakistan is bordered by the two most populous states on earth, China and India. Its western frontier is shared with Afghanistan. The border splits the Pashtuns, 10 million in Afghanistan and 12 million in Pakistan. Islamabad perceives India as the greatest threat to its security. Hence it is imperative to have good relations with Afghanistan and, if possible, China.

THE BORDER SPLITS THE PASHTUNS, 10 MILLION IN AFGHANISTAN AND 12 MILLION IN PAKISTAN.

A major problem for Pakistani–Indian relations is Kashmir, administered by India but claimed by Pakistan. In mid-1999, Pakistan-based Muslim militants penetrated Kashmir and the man who was pulling the strings was perceived to be General Pervez Musharraf. This gave him the aura of being a hard-line Muslim military leader. In July 1999, US pressure and worldwide censure led to a negotiated withdrawal from Kashmir. Washington was mindful of the fact that Pakistan and India are nuclear powers and was concerned that the conflict could escalate and lead to nuclear and missile proliferation. It could also feed the ambitions of Islamic militants and terrorists.

In October 1999, as chief of the army staff, he ordered the overthrow of the unpopular civilian government of Nawaz Sharif, who had been elected in February 1997. The economic situation was very difficult. After some initial hesitation the US government came to terms with General Musharraf. He was the best guarantee against Pakistan dissolving into anarchy and civil disturbance.

Relations with China

Pakistan benefited from the lack of accord between the Soviet Union and China. India was always more important for Moscow so Islamabad naturally sought to improve relations with China. Two border wars were fought between India and China but there are no territorial conflicts between Islamabad and Beijing. China has supplied Pakistan with nuclear technology as well as M-11 ballistic missiles which are capable of delivering nuclear weapons. China has a keen strategic interest in improving relations with Pakistan as it is seeking a friendly port in the Arabian Sea. A plan to develop a deep-water port at Gwadar has been revealed. China may commit up to US$1 billion to fashion a port which will welcome ships of the Chinese Navy.

> CHINA HAS SUPPLIED PAKISTAN WITH NUCLEAR TECHNOLOGY AND MISSILES CAPABLE OF DELIVERING NUCLEAR WEAPONS.

The Taliban

Pakistan's Inter-Services Intelligence (ISI) was influential in ensuring that the bulk of the US–Saudi aid to the mujahidin fighting the Soviets until 1989 was channelled through the Hezb-i-Islam group, headed by the Pashtun, Golbuddin Hekmatyar. However, after the Soviets left, Pakistan's relations with the mujahidin encountered some turbulence. As a consequence, the ISI provided support during the formation of the Taliban, in 1994. By 2001, the Taliban was in control of most of the country. This allowed Pakistan to play a more influential role in Kabul but it led to increasing tensions with the US and Iran. UN sanctions imposed

BY 2001, THE TALIBAN WAS IN CONTROL OF MOST OF THE COUNTRY.

on the Taliban led to Pakistan moderating its position.

Central Asia

Pakistan rushed in after the collapse of communism in 1989. However it made little impact on the region partly because it had no historic roots there. Support for the Taliban alienated the secular Islamic states and Uzbekistan, for example, was quite hostile. Russia, in 2001, was preparing to deploy about 50,000 troops to prevent the Taliban penetrating Central Asia. The events of 11 September removed the need to do this. Pakistan needs the oil and natural gas which Central Asian states can export. However, it needs peace to prevail before the necessary pipelines are built across Afghanistan. There are those who believe that Russia, India and Iran would like to restrict Pakistani influence in Afghanistan and possibly prevent the building of the pipelines. Iran has an interest in ensuring the pipelines to the Persian Gulf go through its territory. Russia wants oil to flow through its pipelines.

Pakistan expects some reward for supporting the US-led attack on Afghanistan. It may come in debt relief and aid rather than in an increase in influence in Afghanistan and Central Asia.

PAKISTAN EXPECTS SOME REWARD FOR SUPPORTING THE US-LED ATTACK ON AFGHANISTAN.

FIVE

11 SEPTEMBER 2001
AND ALL THAT

AFGHANISTAN

The United States has now come to accept Russia's perception of Afghanistan. So alarmed was Moscow in 1979 by the
mounting influence of Muslim clerics and their followers that
it launched its ill-fated invasion in a vain attempt to defeat
the spiritual magnetism of Islam by military means. They
suffered from two great weaknesses: they were foreigners and
they had only a secular vision of the world to supplant Islam.
The Soviets promised greater material wealth, the mullahs
promised spiritual self-fulfilment based on material self-
denial. Moscow took it for granted that modernisation or secularisation was what all developing countries needed. It was
so self-evident there was no need to justify it. Marxism borrowed its economic goals from capitalism. They both shared
the same goal: plenitude on earth. Different routes would be
taken to the promised land: capitalism would bank on individual initiative and endeavour and communism would get
there collectively. There was no third way: there was no
Islamic way. Both the capitalist and communist models left

THE CAPITALIST AND COMMUNIST MODELS LEFT OUT A VITAL INGREDIENT: THE SPIRITUAL DIMENSION.

out a vital ingredient: the spiritual dimension. Religion is a private matter in capitalist countries. Everyone is free to seek his or her own spiritual salvation. To underline this there are over 33,000 different versions of Christianity. Under communism, the spiritual dimension was suppressed. The new Soviet man and woman did not need the prop of religion. In modern capitalist countries the state and religion are separate. Economic and political decisions are normally taken without consulting the churches, indeed any spiritual authority. For many, one's spiritual life is private and should not impinge on one's secular role in society.

This is totally alien to Islam. The latter does not make a distinction between the spiritual and the secular; they form an indissoluble unity. If one examines all the reform proposals

ISLAM DOES NOT MAKE A DISTINCTION BETWEEN THE SPIRITUAL AND THE SECULAR; THEY FORM AN INDISSOLUBLE UNITY.

extended by the capitalists and communists during the last century, not a single one addressed the spiritual dimension of reform. They all focused on the material and assumed that the religious dimension was not their concern. The most extreme version of this was the communist panacea which began to gain converts from the early 1970s onwards. Indeed Afghan communists delighted in insulting the mullahs and the religious sensibilities of the average citizen. Why did the new Afghan leadership adopt such an aggressive policy towards Islam? One would have thought that they would proceed with great caution given the underdevelopment of the country. One of the answers may have been the arrogance of converts. They believed that they possessed the truth and dismissed any criticism as obscurantism. Another factor was the need of the two main factions to compete for the allegiance of members and attract new blood to their cause. Moderation in these circumstances is the route to defeat. The more intense the struggle the greater the radicalism. They all assumed that Soviet military power would protect them from any counter-revolution. It never occurred to them that the mullahs, in their eyes yesterday's men, could actually defeat them and drive them from the land.

So the mullahs took over. They had a charismatic leader in Mullah Omar and his alliance with Osama bin Laden's al-Qaeda soon made them, on paper, impregnable. The same disease of over-confidence quickly afflicted the mullahs

THE MULLAHS CAME TO BELIEVE THEY COULD CHANGE THE WORLD OUTSIDE AFGHANISTAN. THAT WAS A FATAL MISTAKE BUT IT MAY NOT BE TERMINAL.

and their followers. With Allah on their side, could any infidel resist them? They came to believe they could change the world outside Afghanistan. That was a fatal mistake but it may not be terminal. Afghanistan is now preparing to turn over another page of its history. The capitalists, communists and mullahs have all held sway and been swept away. This is a chastening lesson for any new Afghan administration. The way is open for a secular state once

IT WOULD APPEAR THAT THE ONLY WAY FORWARD IS A SECULAR–SPIRITUAL PARTNERSHIP.

again in Afghanistan. Previous ones failed because they did not factor in the spiritual dimension. It would appear that the only way forward is a secular–spiritual partnership.

11 SEPTEMBER 2001

The images of aircraft flying deliberately into the Twin Towers of the World Trade Center, in New York, will remain for ever with those who witnessed them live. These pictures were then compounded by those of the attack on the Pentagon and of the crashed aircraft in Pennsylvania. These events changed American security perceptions for ever. The only time the national territory of the United States has ever been attacked was when the British burned down Washington DC in 1814. On 7 December 1941, Japan attacked Pearl Harbor but it was not the mainland. Hawaii was a Territory, not a State. So 11 September 2001 was a traumatic shock and it came from within. Ground Zero will remain a permanent cemetery for the 2,787 who were incinerated there. Future tourists will be told by guides that that is where America's war against international terrorism, which continues, all began.

THESE EVENTS CHANGED AMERICAN SECURITY PERCEPTIONS FOR EVER.

The first phone call that President George W. Bush received was from a shocked President Vladimir Putin of Russia. 'We are with you', was the gist of Putin's remarks during an emotional exchange of views. Russia was on side. The previous ganging up with China to lambast America was forgotten. Russia and America were part of the Christian world – both Presidents go

to church. The terror-
ists, members of
Osama bin Laden's al-
Qaeda network were
Islamic fundamental-

**RUSSIA WAS ON SIDE. RUSSIA AND
AMERICA WERE PART OF THE CHRISTIAN
WORLD – BOTH PRESIDENTS GO TO
CHURCH.**

ists. They were members of a faith about which the Presidents
knew little, especially President Bush. Afghanistan was the
centre of the terrorist network. Russia knew a lot about the
country and it was all bad. Support for Afghan communists
from 1973 to 1979, followed by military intervention, had all
been a costly mistake. The Soviets learned the hard way that
the Afghans hate foreigners in the country. Those who come
bearing gifts are killed or expelled. The British interventions in
the nineteenth century and the Soviet in the twentieth were
remarkable in that the supposedly backward Afghans beat
leading world powers. The latter were infinitely better armed
than the Afghans but nevertheless succumbed. These thoughts
were rushing through Vladimir Putin's mind as he talked about
what was to come next. All his military and intelligence advisers warned him about getting involved in the Afghan quagmire
– anyone who intervened would lose.

Putin unequivocally supported operation Enduring Freedom
when it was launched. He was pleased that President Bush
underlined that the fight was not against Islam, it was not a
modern version of the Crusades but a struggle against international terrorism.
This was important
for Russia's 20 million
Muslims, one in seven
of the population.

**PRESIDENT BUSH UNDERLINED THAT THE
FIGHT WAS NOT A MODERN VERSION OF
THE CRUSADES BUT A STRUGGLE
AGAINST INTERNATIONAL TERRORISM.**

When the bombing began on 7 October, Russian Muslims did not see it that way. Geydar Dzhemel, head of the Russian interregional Islamic committee, immediately reacted. He claimed that the attacks on 11 September had been planned 'by anti-Islamic forces trying to destabilise the world situation, no matter who technically carried out the attacks'. Russian Muslims, according to the cleric, should regard the American bombing of Afghanistan as a direct attack on them. These attacks, he claimed, would 'widen the abyss which separated the Russian leadership from the multi-million Muslim population'. Putin had been warned not to participate physically in the US war in Afghanistan. The good news for Putin was that by late October about 60 per cent of Russians supported US bombing. Compared to Putin, George Bush had a smooth ride. Americans wanted revenge.

COMPARED TO PUTIN, GEORGE BUSH HAD A SMOOTH RIDE. AMERICANS WANTED REVENGE.

PUTIN'S GAME

The Russian President seized his opportunity to come in from the cold and to start building a strategic alliance with the only world superpower, the US. He took the initiative without consulting his military, intelligence and foreign policy communities. Sergei Ivanov, the defence minister made it quite clear that Russia was not going to become involved and would not open its air space. The chief of the general staff, General Anatoly Kvashnin, made similar noises. On 24 September, after talking for 40 minutes with George Bush, Putin put flesh on the details. Intelligence cooperation and sharing (Russian military intelligence, GRU, has the best intelligence-gathering network in Afghanistan and Iran); Russian airspace to be open to humanitarian aid; cooperation with Central Asian states to prepare their airfields to do the same – then Sergei Ivanov added that they would also be got ready for military operations – one of the fastest retreats and advances in recent military history; participation in international search and rescue missions; and direct military assistance to the Northern Alliance which would include weapons, equipment and advisers. Not even under Boris Yeltsin had Russia gone this far. Opening up Russian and Central Asian airspace was a dramatic departure from past suspicion and hostility. If Putin was taking these risks he must have received something tangible in return. He did in the form of the US completely reversing its stance on Chechnya. Washington now called on President Maskhadov to sever links with international terrorism. Chechnya and Afghanistan were now on a par: international terrorism was the chief enemy in both places.

> OPENING UP RUSSIAN AND CENTRAL ASIAN AIRSPACE WAS A DRAMATIC DEPARTURE FROM PAST SUSPICION AND HOSTILITY.

Predictably the Russian communists thought the whole idea of a pact with America against international terrorism was a conspiracy to weaken Russia. Vladimir Zhirinovsky, Mad Vlad to some of his friends, can always be guaranteed to come up with a colourful quote. 'NATO needs Russia as an outpost. We shall sweat and bleed on the borders of the Muslim world ... Soldiers and military hardware will be Russian. NATO may accept that now because it is afraid. As far as NATO is concerned the situation is out of control. Why is Russia in the war? To have its foreign debts written off.' So far he has been wide of the mark.

In late September, Putin travelled to Germany and became the first Russian leader to address the Bundestag, the German parliament, in Berlin, in German. He also pleased the other western industrialised countries. He announced that Russia would increase its oil exports if sources in the Middle East were cut off by political or military action. Later he stated that Russia was closing its tracking station in Lourdes, Cuba – much to the chagrin of President Castro – and its naval base at Cam Ranh, Vietnam. The Russians had about 1,000 personnel in Cuba.

US SECRET ALLIANCE IN CENTRAL ASIA

Covert operations are very attractive to American Presidents. If they are successful, they can take the credit. If they fail, they can be denied. America's covert mission in Central Asia began in 1998 in Uzbekistan. Two events provoked it. The Taliban offensive of February 1998, which routed the Uzbek-backed General Abdul Rashid Dostum, and brought the Taliban right up to the 125 km Uzbek–Afghan border. The other was the bombing of the US embassies in Kenya and Tanzania, in August 1998. The goal was to

> COVERT OPERATIONS ARE VERY ATTRACTIVE TO AMERICAN PRESIDENTS. IF THEY ARE SUCCESSFUL, THEY CAN TAKE THE CREDIT. IF THEY FAIL, THEY CAN BE DENIED.

strengthen the Northern Alliance (NA) and weaken Osama bin Laden's network, which was identified as the source of the attacks. US Special Forces began working with the Uzbek military on training missions. Uzbekistan was the first Central Asian state publicly to express support for a US military operation in Afghanistan. On 5 October, President Islam Karimov told Donald Rumsfeld, in Tashkent, that the Americans could station ground troops, aircraft and helicopters in local air bases. Uzbekistan's reward was in hard cash. The country wants the US to help it solve its difficult economic problems. This in turn will strengthen Uzbekistan's bid for leadership of the Central Asian region. It has various territorial claims on southern Kazakhstan and could play this card. Kazakhstan is feeling left out of the struggle with Afghanistan. Russia has recently told Kazakhstan to support the Russian position of dividing up the Caspian Sea, if it wants a larger share.

In early 2002 the US was putting flesh on its ambitions to extend its power to countries previously outside its reach. A permanent American base has been established at Khanabad, Uzbekistan, which will house 1,500 personnel. In neighbouring Kyrgyzstan, at Manas, near Bishkek, the capital, a transport hub is being created which will have 3,000 soldiers, warplanes and surveillance aircraft. Other airfields are being used in Tajikistan. The US has begun to rotate its troops in the region, thus institutionalising a previously temporary arrangement.

The reward for this cooperation is hard cash and military training for the local military. Uzbekistan received $64 million in US aid and $136 million in US Export–Import Bank credits in 2001. In 2002, $52 million in assistance has been promised to Kazakhstan, some of it for military equipment. The poor human rights record in the area has been overlooked in the search for strategic allies. The war against terrorism sweeps aside every other consideration.

THE POOR HUMAN RIGHTS RECORD IN THE AREA HAS BEEN OVERLOOKED IN THE SEARCH FOR STRATEGIC ALLIES.

RUSSIAN AID DECISIVE

There was a division of labour between America and Russia in the war against the Taliban. The US would bomb the Taliban infrastructure and the Russians would equip, train and aid the NA. Washington would pay for the new hardware. The ground attacks were to be coordinated with the air strikes. The last time this level of military cooperation between Washington and Moscow occurred was 1945. Russian-equipped Uzbek and Tajik special forces joined the NA and were successful in clashes with the Taliban. The Russians provided dozens of T-55 tanks, sometimes with Russian crews, and armoured personnel carriers, as well as munitions. Russian military matériel and advisors turned the tide in the war against the Taliban militia.

THE US WOULD BOMB THE TALIBAN INFRASTRUCTURE AND THE RUSSIANS WOULD EQUIP, TRAIN AND AID THE NA.

A month after US bombing began, the NA had hardly advanced at all. The US concentrated on taking out Taliban command and control centres and other targets. It did not seem to make any difference and there was gloomy talk of a winter campaign. The NA, only 15,000 strong, was confronted by a Taliban army of about 50,000, which included thousands of al-Qaeda fighters. The latter were mainly non-Afghan – Pakistanis, Chechens, Chinese Uighurs, Arabs from various countries and some British and other European Muslims. They would not surrender. When their bullets ran out they committed suicide by exploding their own hand grenades.

> **THEY WOULD NOT SURRENDER. WHEN THEIR BULLETS RAN OUT THEY COMMITTED SUICIDE BY EXPLODING THEIR OWN HAND GRENADES.**

The intensive American bombing of the Taliban infrastructure continued as long as Washington judged that the NA was not capable militarily of defeating the Taliban. Once the NA had been reequipped and was capable of launching a successful offensive, the Americans switched to destroying concentrations of Taliban militia facing the NA. It was thought that large-scale losses would demoralise Taliban forces and that the NA could then attack successfully. The policy change occurred on 1 November when Taliban fighters outside Kabul came under intense bombardment. Mazar-e Sharif was also hit. The next day, Washington considered that the NA could soon advance to Kabul. Another reason for the delay in hitting Taliban militia from the air was the desire to have a viable coalition government ready when Kabul fell. The change in tactics meant that had gone by the board. The NA could now move to take Mazar-e Sharif. Another important asset for the Americans was that the Russians provided them with a superabundance of intelligence on the Taliban, al-Qaeda leaders, detailed information on the tribal chiefs, local history, paths and sources of water. The flood of information amazed the American intelligence community.

All did not go to plan. The NA commanders gave assurances that they would advance but not enter Kabul. This promise was broken when troops of General Muhammad Fahim Khan, the successor to General Ahmad Shah Masoud, murdered by the Taliban in September 2001, drove in triumph into the capital. All their tanks and other equipment were Russian. When Kunduz fell in late November, NA forces were, more or less, in control of 60 per cent of the country. That is to say, Afghan Tajiks and Uzbeks were in control. The Russians flew in a government delegation to Kabul, brought in tonnes of humanitarian aid and began building a field hospital and embassy in Kabul, all before the end of November. On paper, Vladimir Putin has succeeded in reestablishing Russian influence in Afghanistan. All his predecessors, from Leonid Brezhnev to Boris Yeltsin had failed. However, real Russian influence ends at Kabul. The southern part of the country, mainly Pashtun territory, is beyond their reach. American and British forces did contribute to the taking of Kandahar, the Taliban capital, but the main fighting was done by various anti-Taliban groups. The Taliban and al-Qaeda surrendered, much to the surprise of some observers who had expected them to fight to the death. Then began the conflict among the various anti-Taliban

THE NA COMMANDERS GAVE ASSURANCES THAT THEY WOULD ADVANCE BUT NOT ENTER KABUL. THIS PROMISE WAS BROKEN.

groups for suprem-
acy in Kandahar.
The various Pashtun
tribes could not
agree. Given the

THE TALIBAN AND AL-QAEDA
SURRENDERED, MUCH TO THE SURPRISE OF
SOME OBSERVERS WHO HAD EXPECTED
THEM TO FIGHT TO THE DEATH.

experiences of 1992–96, this was entirely predictable.

Is Russia just a member of the allied coalition or is it imple-
menting its own carefully thought-out policy? The latter is
the case. Putin put General Anatoly Kvashnin in charge of
Afghan operations. He appointed Sergei Shoigu, a close con-
fidant, to supervise Russia's $500 million humanitarian assist-
ance programme in northern Afghanistan. Choosing such a
high-profile politician as Shoigu reflected the importance
Putin ascribed to the Afghan problem. While at a summit
with George Bush, in Texas, Putin mentioned that the seizure
of Kabul had not come as a surprise to the Russians. It was a
goal which we 'set ourselves at the first stage – the liberation
of northern Afghanistan – and then Kabul'. Immediately
after taking charge of Russian military assistance to the
NA, General Kvashnin, and the deputy head of the Federal
Security Service (FSB) – the successor to the KGB – met NA
military leaders in Dushanbe, Tajikistan. By early October
Russian military hardware was rolling into Afghanistan.
Ironically, Kvashnin is one of the few senior Russian military
officers who did not serve in Afghanistan, between 1979 and
1989. However, he commanded Russian troops in Kosovo, in
1999, and this provided him with important experience of
working with a US-backed coalition. He demonstrated that
he could outfox the Americans. He led the lightning advance
which seized Pristina under the noses of the allies, towards

the end of the Balkan war. His influence appears to have been decisive in the NA decision to occupy Kabul.

Another important asset from the Russian point of view is General Muhammad Fahim Khan, the NA's military commander and a Tajik. A former intelligence officer, trained by the Russians (KGB), he was once an officer in KHAD, the Soviet-trained Afghan communist secret police. He was a deputy to Najibullah, who continued in power after 1989. He stayed with the communist government until it fell in 1992. Then he joined mujahidin forces commanded by Ahmed Shah Masoud. He is an asset to the Russians because of his intelligence and military links but also because he appears to be deeply hostile to Pakistan. Pakistan's Inter-Service Intelligence (ISI) suspect that he organised the attack on the Pakistani embassy in Kabul, in 1996. He was then the chief of security of the NA when it ruled the Afghan capital from 1992 to 1996.

What does Fahim Khan gain from close cooperation with the Russians? Moscow backed the NA in its attempts to be recognised as the government of Afghanistan. Russian officials are building an embassy in Kabul and other Russian diplomats have reopened their consulate in Mazar-e Sharif. After announcing that Russia was sending a high-level delegation to Kabul, Sergei Ivanov, minister of defence, called the NA the 'legitimate government of Afghanistan'. Hence Moscow does not appear to have much interest in a broad-based coalition government in Kabul wielding real power. The NA and Russia have much to gain from close collaboration. Putin made it clear from the beginning that he would oppose mod-

erate Taliban partici-
pation in an Afghan
coalition government.

THE NA AND RUSSIA HAVE MUCH TO GAIN FROM CLOSE COLLABORATION.

Pakistan is the main supporter of the Pashtuns. Russia is forging a new India–Iran–Russia strategic partnership, the object of which is to encircle Pakistan. The latter was the main sponsor of the Taliban which caused so many security headaches for Moscow. There was even a risk that the Taliban would penetrate Central Asia and, in so doing, become a source of inspiration for Russia's Muslims. Pakistan hopes to gain access to Central Asian oil and gas supplies, a tangible reward for backing the US. The new partnership is attractive to Iran as it increases security on its eastern border and affords some influence over the evolution of Afghanistan.

THE US AND OIL

The US National Intelligence Service recently prepared a report on world developments until 2015. It concluded that the greatest increase in demand for energy would be in China and India. This means that by 2015 only one tenth of the oil produced in the Persian Gulf region will go to the western market. Iran and Iraq are not likely to reverse their present stance and become friendly to Washington. After the initial air strikes against Afghanistan, Saudi Arabia broke off diplomatic relations with the US. The country with the largest hydrocarbon reserves can no longer be regarded as a reliable American ally. This adds strategic significance to the oil reserves of the Caspian Sea basin. They are the third largest outside Russia and the Middle East. America has to ensure that oil flows from the region to the west. No terrorist group can be permitted to interrupt these supplies.

Russia and the newly independent states together produce about one tenth of the world's oil and about one third of its natural gas. Russian oil industry is booming. In December 2001, production began in a northern gas field with reserves equal to two thirds of those of the rest of Europe. Kazakhstan hopes to double output by 2010. Non-Middle East oil is becoming more attractive by the day. Until now Russia and the west have been competing to build pipelines to carry the black gold to western markets. Now Russia and America can compete commercially to get the oil out. Russia is no longer trying to block the Baku–Ceyhan pipeline. It believes that it can compete successfully with it.

NON-MIDDLE EAST OIL IS BECOMING MORE ATTRACTIVE BY THE DAY.

In 2001, Russia was producing about 7 million barrels a day compared to Saudi Arabia's 8.4 million. It was exporting 2.8 million barrels a day but this was nowhere near the 7.1 million of Saudi Arabia. Plans for new Russian pipelines would add another 2.5 million barrels a day but work has not yet begun. It will take five to ten years to have them fully operational. However the first stage of the new Baltic pipeline system was completed by the end of 2001. It will carry oil from the Pechora region to Primorsk, on the Gulf of Finland, but only 240,000 export barrels a day. At present America imports about 2.5 million barrels a day from the Persian Gulf. Russia's oil reserves are over 50 billion barrels but there is more oil in Siberia to be discovered. Central Asia may have

110 billion barrels. This is still small compared to Saudi Arabia's 262 billion barrels. The message is clear. If Russia and Central Asia remain stable over the next five to ten years, the region can end America's need for Gulf oil.

The consequences of the coming oil boom are enormous for Central Asia. The hydrocarbon countries will become richer and the authoritarian leaders almost impregnable. The American pursuit of

THE CONSEQUENCES OF THE COMING OIL BOOM ARE ENORMOUS FOR CENTRAL ASIA.

democracy and a liberal market economy in Central Asia has borne almost no fruit. These aspirations will now be pushed into the background as America helps the region to export more oil and gas. Of course, in the longer term, these countries would become more prosperous if they adopted more liberal policies. However, the leaderships would prefer no opposition to their rule. Democracy would topple them. Most people in Central Asia at present are miserably poor. Even with the Taliban defeated, many will feel that the Islamic way forward offers them more than the present situation.

THE END OF THE TALIBAN?

After nine days of talks in Bonn, Germany, Afghan anti-Taliban groups signed an agreement on a 30-minister interim government on 5 December 2001. The difficult task of awarding portfolios ended

AFGHAN ANTI-TALIBAN GROUPS SIGNED AN AGREEMENT ON A 30-MINISTER INTERIM GOVERNMENT ON 5 DECEMBER 2001.

with 11of them going to the Pashtuns. The Tajiks got eight, the Uzbeks three and the Hazaras five. Hence the NA did best of all. Even better from a Tajik perspective, the most crucial posts, defence, internal affairs and foreign affairs have gone to them. A Pashtun, Hamid Karzai, was elected chair of the interim administration. He is head of one of the tribes which make up the Pashtun ethnic group. He is an anti-Taliban leader and helped to deliver covert US aid to the mujahidin when they were fighting the Soviets between 1979 and 1989. Three of his brothers live in the US and Washington supplied Karzai with ammunition and food in his battle with the Taliban this autumn.

Of the five vice-chairs, one is a woman: Sima Samar, who is Hazara. The other four include the key post of minister of defence and this goes to Fahim Khan, who is commander-in-chief of the NA. The interim administration assumed office on 22 December 2001. The UN provided a multinational force to secure Kabul and the surrounding areas. The interim administration will reestablish the legal system and a commission to convene a Loya Jirga, or council of tribal elders.

Under the guidance of Zahir Shah, the former king, the Loya Jirga will meet to select an authority to hold power for two years. The new

THE INTERIM ADMINISTRATION WILL REESTABLISH THE LEGAL SYSTEM AND A COMMISSION TO CONVENE A LOYA JIRGA, OR COUNCIL OF TRIBAL ELDERS.

transitional authority will assume office on 22 June 2002. A constitutional Loya Jirga will convene to agree a new constitution and a date for a general election in 2004.

This is an extremely ambitious timetable for the new

Afghanistan. Given the inter-tribal and inter-ethnic rivalries of the country it is entirely predictable that there will be conflict, even armed conflict between and among groups. General Dostum, the Uzbek warlord whose base is Mazar-e Sharif, stated immediately after the signing ceremony that he would not work with the new authority. Evidently he wants a larger share of the cake. There is to be an international conference of donors, in January 2002, in Japan, to discuss the reconstruction of Afghanistan. If $10 billion is put on the table, it can be used as bait in an attempt to get the various groups to cooperate. If $5 billion goes to the NA and the other $5 billion to the Pashtuns this will make the warlords very powerful.

IF $5 BILLION GOES TO THE NA AND THE OTHER $5 BILLION TO THE PASHTUNS THIS WILL MAKE THE WARLORDS VERY POWERFUL.

Afghanistan is facing a de facto division between north and south. The Uzbek and Tajik warlords in the north are seeking to consolidate their power and establish fiefdoms. At their backs are the Russians. International aid will contribute greatly to their power. The Pashtuns in the south have to agree among themselves on the division of the spoils. If the Pashtuns feel resentment at the post-war settlement the ground will have been laid for the reemergence of a new fighting force to remedy the situation. This would be Taliban Mark II. Many Taliban and al-Qaeda fighters have made their way into Pakistan to regroup, reform and plan how to continue their fight for a Wahhabbi Islamic Afghanistan. There are many young Pashtuns who are keen to continue the struggle. There are about 22 million Pashtuns divided between Afghanistan and Pakistan. Hence recruits are not difficult to find. The best defence against the resurgence of another version of the Taliban would be the desire of Afghan Pashtuns to bid farewell to the struggle to take over Afghanistan and impose Wahhabi Islam. They need to believe that peace will bring them greater dividends than war. Thus the peace settlement and the financial rewards which will flow from it are crucial for the evolution of a peaceful Afghanistan.

AFGHAN PASHTUNS NEED TO BELIEVE THAT PEACE WILL BRING THEM GREATER DIVIDENDS THAN WAR.

This said, the remnants of the Taliban and al-Qaeda are not interested in the reconstruction of Afghanistan if it marginalises them. Available evidence points to the fact that captured Taliban fighters and their leaders are not being handed over to the Americans. This is taking place in Pashtun-dominated territory. Already local tribal leaders are fashioning their own agenda and it does not include acceding to US wishes on a range of issues. Will these Taliban fighters form the backbone of a Pashtun military force to rival those of the northern warlords? The interim administration is weak. Afghan experience points to someone trying to become the new strongman of the country. Is this the future for the country?

CAPTURED TALIBAN FIGHTERS AND THEIR LEADERS ARE NOT BEING HANDED OVER TO THE AMERICANS.

GUIDE TO FURTHER READING

More is now being written about Afghanistan and Central Asia than ever before. Indeed there are many books in the pipeline and such has been the pace of events in the last months of 2001 that most of them may be out of date when published. The writing on Afghanistan has been dominated lately by the Taliban and al-Qaeda. *Taliban* by Ahmed Rashid (Pan, 2001) provided essential background to the conflict there. *The Taliban* by Peter Marsden (Zed Books, 1998) covers the early years of the Taliban advance in Afghanistan. *The New Jackals: Osama bin Laden and the Future of Terrorism* by Simon Reeve (André Deutsch, 2001) provides background on America's public enemy number 1. There has been a flood of intelligence information on bin Laden released by the Americans and others. On the historical background and insights into the reasons why Afghanistan became a failed state, see Martin Ewans, *Afghanistan: A New History* (Curzon Press, 2001).

There are some excellent surveys of various aspects of Central Asian affairs, notably Ahmed Rashid, *The Resurgence of Central Asia* (Zed Books, 1994); Jacob M. Landau and Barbara Kellner-Heinkele *Politics of Language in the Ex-Soviet Muslim States* (Hurst, 2001); Graham Smith *et al.*, *Nation Building in the Post-Soviet Borderlands* (Cambridge University Press, 1998); M. Holt Ruffin (ed.), *Civil Society in Central Asia* (University of Washington Press, 1999); Akira Miyamoto, *Natural Gas in Central Asia: Industries, Markets, Export Options of Kazakhstan, Turkmenistan and Uzbekistan* (Royal Institute of International Relations, 1998). An important aspect of the region is the Soviet legacy and this is well covered by John Glenn, *The Soviet Legacy in Central Asia* (Palgrave, 1999). On the international politics and security of Central Asia see John Anderson, *The International Politics of Central Asia* (Manchester University Press, 1997) and Roy Allison and Lena Jonson (eds), *Central Asian Security: The New International Context* (Royal Institute of International Affairs, 2001). The latter is especially timely and thoughtful. A very useful background book to the region is Karen Dawisha and Bruce Parrott, *Russia and the New States of Eurasia: The Politics of Upheaval* (Cambridge University Press, 1994). Economics is covered in

Tajikistan, Turkmenistan and Uzbekistan (European Bank for Reconstruction and Development Stationery Office, 1999). Martin McCauley, *Investing in the Caspian Sea Region: Opportunity and Risk* (Catermill, 1996) provides background information on today's problems and options.

There is some first-class literature on the individual countries. On Kazakhstan see Sally Cummings, *Centre-Periphery Relations in Kazakhstan* (The Brookings Institution, 2000); Armin Bauer *et al.*, *Women and Gender relations in Kazakhstan: The Social Cost* (Asian Development Bank, 1997). On Uzbekistan the indispensable guide is Edward A. Allworth, *The Modern Uzbeks: From the 14th Century to the Present: A Cultural History* (Hoover Institution Press, 1989). Other illuminating publications on Uzbekistan are Annette Bohr, *Uzbekistan: Politics and Foreign Policy* (Royal Institute of International Affairs, 1998); Neil J. Melvin, *Uzbekistan* (Harwood Academic, 2000); Nancy Lubin *et al.*, analyse a crucial area in *Calming the Ferghana Valley: Development and Dialogue in the Heart of Central Asia* (The Brookings Institution, 2000). The best guide to Kyrgyzstan is John Anderson, *Kyrgyzstan: Central Asia's Island of Democracy?* (Harwood Academic, 1999). On Tajikistan see Shirin Akiner, *Tajikstan* (The Brookings Institution, 1998). The International Monetary Fund's report on Tajikstan is published by the Stationery Office (2001). Catch a fascinating glimpse of Turkmenistan in Carole Blackwell, *Tradition in Society in Turkmenistan: Gender, Oral Culture and Song* (Curzon Press, 2001).

On Soviet nationality policy Hélène Carrère d'Encausse, *The Great Challenge: Nationalities and the Bolshevik State 1917–1930* (Holmes & Meier, 1992), is outstanding. On Islam her work is also of great significance. *Islam and the Russian Empire: Reform and the Revolution in Central Asia* (I.B. Tauris, 1988) examines in illuminating detail Bukhara from the Russian Conquest to 1917. A finely researched and hugely informative analysis of Islam after 1945 is Yaacov Ro'i, *Islam in the Soviet Union: From World War II to Perestroika* (Hurst, 2000).

INDEX

INDEX